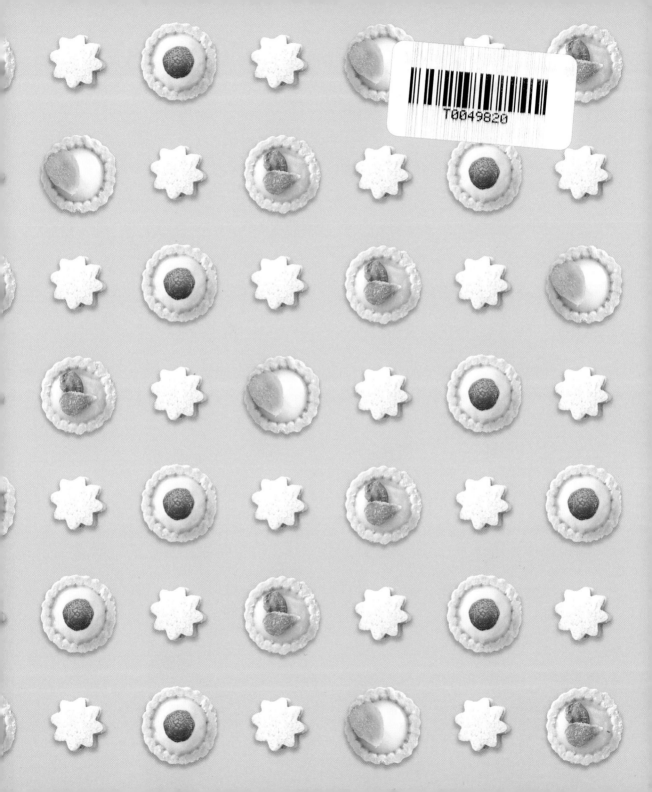

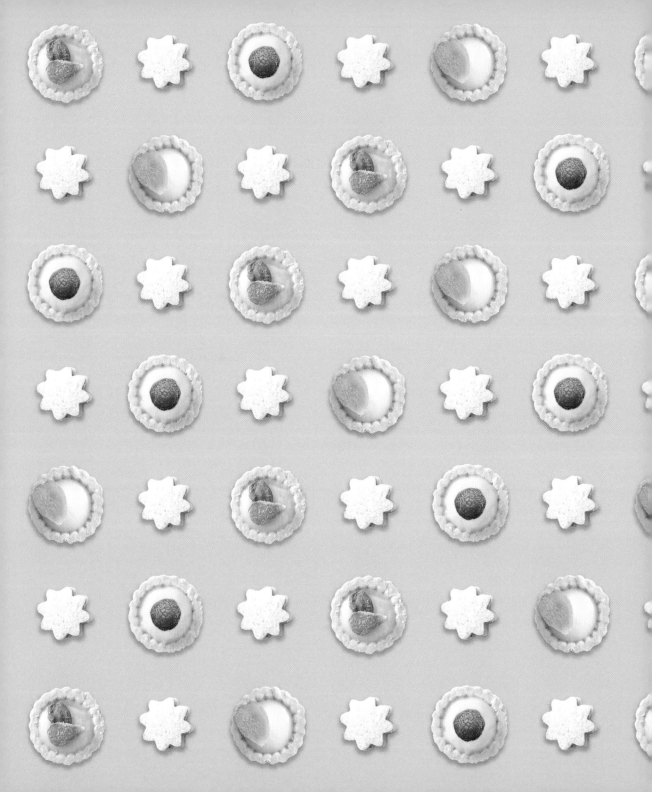

American Girl®

Tea Parties

weldon**owen**

Contents

Savory Snacks

Drinks

Basics

It's Teatime!

All around the world, the daily ritual of teatime is a revered tradition, especially when it means bringing together your friends or family members. From Japan to China to India to Britain, teatime is an occasion to eat tasty food, enjoy delicious drinks, and spend some fun time together. In these pages, you'll find loads of recipes for shareable treats and yummy drinks to help you host the perfect tea party. All the classics are here, from scones and tea sandwiches to tartlets and cupcakes, plus a selection of savory treats such as sushi, gougères, and pot pies. When the weather is warm, invite a bunch of pals to an alfresco summer tea bash with Frozen Chai (page 100) and Strawberries & Cream Cupcakes (page 45). Or cozy up on a cold winter day with a warm Apple-Orange Tea (page 109). For an after-school tea gathering, serve Colorful Macarons (page 27) and Mint Tisane (page 105). This collection of recipes and ideas will give you plenty of inspiration to celebrate teatime anytime.

Teatime Prep

When you are planning a tea party for your friends, ask yourself the following questions to get started:

★ Who's invited?

Once you've decided to host a tea party, the first step is to make a guest list. How many people would you like to invite? Remember, the more people you invite, the more planning and prep you will have to do. A handcrafted note explaining the details—what day, what time, what the occasion is—adds a personal touch to your invitation.

★ What's cookin'?

These recipes are designed to delight your friends. Do your chums like chocolate? Fruity desserts? What about savory snacks? Pick several recipes that you think your friends will like. When in doubt, a combination of sweet and savory treats can't be beat. You'll want to prepare as many dishes and decorations ahead of time as you can so that you'll have time to enjoy the fun when the party rolls around.

★ When's the party?

Do you want your next birthday to be a tea-party extravaganza? How about having friends over to hang out after school? Or would you like to host an outdoor party on a summer afternoon? Or a fireside tea party—and sleepover—in winter? The time of year and the weather, as well as upcoming holidays, will help you come up with ideas for the theme, location, colors, and menu. Get creative and have fun!

★ Why teatime?

Imagine your tea party: Are you gathering friends to watch movies together? Or to play in the backyard? Or to craft gifts for the winter holidays? Whatever the occasion, think about what kind of games you'd like to play or activities you'd like to do.

★ Pulling it all together

Staying organized is the key to hosting a fun party—and to enjoying the party yourself! To help you prepare for the occasion, make a checklist of everything you'll need to do beforehand—it will help you keep things running smoothly. Think about what ingredients you'll need for the recipes, supplies you'll want for making party decorations, any party favors you might want to hand out, and what you'll need to set up beforehand. The more you plan and do ahead of time, the more time you'll have for fun!

Tea Party Ideas

You can use the themes below to help you start planning your teatime party—and to create other themes. Feel free to mix and match these themes and dishes—your choice of snacks, decorations, and activities will make for a unique party with your own flair!

SUMMER ALFRESCO

Nothing says a summer party like cool drinks and tasty treats made with produce from a farmers' market. If your party will be in the sunny outdoors, try picking recipes with a rainbow assortment of fruits. Lemon Tartlets with Sugared Flowers (page 33), Watermelon "Layer" Cake (page 77), and Summer Fruit Buttermilk Tart (page 63) make the most of the fresh fruits and berries available. An elegant Garden Flower Sandwich Cake (page 80), Fresh Tomato Tart (page 85), or veggie-filled Rainbow Sushi (page 96) will round out your menu with yummy savory treats. If it's a hot day, a cool Mint Tisane (page 105) or frosty pitcher of Apple-Orange Tea (page 109) will help keep your guests cool.

AFTER-SCHOOL TEA

If you're eager to enjoy an afternoon tea-party play date, or a relaxing Saturday gathering with friends, whip up a few dainty treats to share. You can have fun with a pink-and-orange color theme by serving crispy Colorful Macarons (page 27) with Pink-Orange Tartlets (page 56) and Little Apple Galettes (page 67). A warm teapot filled with Apple-Orange Tea (page 109) or cool glasses of Frozen Chai (page 100) will taste wonderful with these fruity desserts.

COZY CLASSICS

Brush off the winter blues with a teatime party celebrating global snacks and drinks. You may be familiar with Scones with Jam & Cream (page 18) and Cucumber Tea Sandwiches (page 24); they're often served at British teatime. Impress your friends with your knowledge of culinary traditions from around the world by making Hanami Dango (page 35), sweet mochi dumplings popular in Japan. Serve them with Strawberry-Coconut Boba Tea (page 106) for a tasty pairing. Or choose treats from India, like Potato & Pea Samosas (page 88) paired with a spicy Masala Chai (page 102)—perfect for a cold day.

Cooking with Care

The recipes in this book use hot appliances, sharp objects, and raw food ingredients. Making sure you stay safe and healthy in the kitchen should be your number-one priority. Keep these tips handy and always have an adult nearby when in doubt.

Ask an Adult

When you see this symbol in the book, it means that you need an adult to help you with all or part of the recipe. Ask for help before continuing.

Adults have lots of culinary wisdom, and they can help keep you safe in the kitchen. Always have an adult assist you, especially if your recipe involves high heat, sharp objects, and electric appliances. Be sure to wash your hands before you begin cooking and after touching raw meat, poultry, or eggs.

★ Watch the Heat

Stovetop burners, hot ovens, boiling water—there's a lot of heat involved in cooking, so it's important to be careful when working in the kitchen. Always use oven mitts when handling hot equipment, and have an adult help you when you're cooking at the stovetop, moving pans in and out of the oven, and working with hot liquids or foods.

★ Get Help with Sharp Tools

Soon you'll be chopping, slicing, and mincing, but before you start, make sure an adult is there to help you choose the correct knife (not too big, but not too small either), and be sure to hold the knife firmly at the base. When you're not using the knife, place it somewhere safe so it can't fall on the floor or be reached by younger siblings.

★ Stay Organized

Staying organized and paying attention are important cooking skills. Before you fire up the stovetop or oven, read the recipe, including the ingredient list, from start to finish. Then it's time to clear a clean surface and lay out all your cooking tools and ingredients. Once the food starts cooking, be sure to set a timer.

The two most important baking ingredients are attention to detail and imagination. Have fun!

Teatime Classics

Scones with Jam & Cream

Scones are a must-have for a fancy tea party. These fluffy, biscuit-like pastries originated in Scotland and are traditionally served with jam and whipped or clotted cream (a thickened cream found in Britain). The egg wash will give them a golden top.

2 cups all-purpose flour, plus more for dusting

1 tablespoon baking powder

2 teaspoons sugar, plus 1 tablespoon for sprinkling

1 teaspoon salt

1 cup heavy cream

1 large egg white, lightly beaten with 1 teaspoon water

Whipped Cream (page 115)

Strawberry, raspberry, or other berry jam of your choice

Preheat the oven to 425°F. Have an ungreased cookie sheet ready.

In a large bowl, whisk together the flour, baking powder, the 2 teaspoons sugar, and the salt. Using a large spoon, stir in the cream just until combined. Using your hands, gently gather the dough together, kneading it against the side of the bowl until it holds together in a rough ball.

Sprinkle a work surface with flour. Dump the dough onto the floured surface. Using a rolling pin, roll out the dough to about ¾ inch thick. Using a 3-inch round cookie cutter, cut out circles of dough, pressing the cookie cutter straight down and lifting it straight up and spacing the circles as close together as possible. Place the dough rounds at least 2 inches apart on the cookie sheet. Gather up the dough scraps, knead them briefly together on the floured work surface, and roll out the dough again. Cut out more rounds using the cookie cutter, and add them to the cookie sheet.

Using a pastry brush, lightly brush the tops of the rounds with the egg wash, then sprinkle the remaining 1 tablespoon sugar evenly over the tops.

Bake the scones until golden, 10 to 12 minutes. Transfer to a wire rack to cool.

Using a serrated knife, slice the scones in half horizontally. Spread each half with about 1 tablespoon each of whipped cream and jam. Serve warm or at room temperature.

Smooth edges

To create smooth edges and get the best rise, don't twist or wiggle the cookie cutter when cutting out the scones—press it straight down and lift it straight up.

Crumpets

These are just like pancakes but made with yeast (instead of baking soda or baking powder) to help them rise. Ring molds are open metal circles that bakers use to create fancy pastries. You can buy them at cooking-supply stores or online.

3¼ cups all-purpose flour

4 teaspoons salt

½ teaspoon baking soda

2 cups whole milk, 1 cup heated to 115°F and 1 cup at room temperature

2 tablespoons sugar

1 teaspoon active dry yeast

Unsalted butter, for the molds, pan, and serving

Jam, for serving

In a medium bowl, whisk together the flour, salt, and baking soda. In a large bowl, combine the 1 cup heated milk, sugar, and yeast and let stand until foamy, about 10 minutes. With an electric mixer on low speed, slowly add the flour mixture and then the 1 cup room-temperature milk, beating until a smooth, thick batter forms. Cover the bowl loosely with plastic wrap and set in a warm place until the batter expands and becomes bubbly, about 1 hour.

Heat a large cast-iron frying pan or heavy-bottomed skillet over medium heat. While the pan is heating, butter as many 4-inch ring molds as will fit comfortably in the pan. When the pan is hot, lightly grease it with butter, then place the prepared molds in the pan. Fill each ring with about ⅓ cup batter and cook until bubbles appear on the surface, about 6 minutes. Carefully remove the rings and use a spatula to flip the crumpets over. Cook until the crumpets are golden on the second side and cooked through, about 5 minutes. Transfer to a plate and keep warm.

Repeat with the remaining batter, buttering the ring molds each time. Serve hot with butter and jam.

Prince of Wales Biscuits

Cookies are called "biscuits" in Great Britain. These traditional stamped cookies were invented in the early 1800s and are the perfect partners for a cup of tea. You'll need 3-inch cookie stamps, which you can buy online or at craft stores.

2⅓ cups all-purpose flour, plus more for dusting the cookie stamps

½ teaspoon salt

¾ cup (1½ sticks) cold unsalted butter, diced

½ cup sugar

1 large egg

1 teaspoon vanilla extract

 Preheat the oven to 350°F. Line 2 cookie sheets with parchment paper.

In a medium bowl, whisk together the flour and salt. In a large bowl, using an electric mixer, beat the butter on medium speed until smooth, about 1 minute. Add the sugar, raise the speed to medium-high, and beat until fluffy and lighter in color, 2 to 3 minutes. Add the egg and vanilla and beat until fully incorporated. On medium-low speed, add the flour mixture and beat just until blended.

Put a few spoonfuls of flour in a small, shallow bowl to use for dusting the cookie stamps. Using your hands, shape the dough into 1½-inch balls—about the size of a golf ball—and set aside on a work surface. Working with 6 dough balls at a time, dip half of each ball into the flour to coat the upper half lightly and arrange the balls, flour side up and about 3 inches apart, on a prepared cookie sheet. Lightly flour a 3-inch cookie stamp and gently but firmly flatten the dough ball until the dough reaches the edges of the stamp (any excess can be trimmed away with the tip of a knife). Carefully lift off the stamp. Repeat the flouring and pressing step with the remaining dough balls, arranging them on the cookie sheets.

Bake one sheet at a time (slide the remaining cookie sheet into the refrigerator if the kitchen is warm) until the cookies are light golden brown around the edges (the bottoms will be darker than the edges), 15 to 17 minutes. Repeat to bake the remaining cookies. Let the cookies cool on the cookie sheet on a wire rack for 10 minutes, then serve.

Best fresh
These cookies are best when served on the day you bake them.

Cucumber Tea Sandwiches

There's no dish that says tea party more than yummy tea sandwiches! All you'll need are a cucumber, some butter, some bread, and a sprinkle of salt and pepper. Don't forget to cut off the crusts so they're extra dainty.

1 English cucumber, thinly sliced

Salt and ground black pepper

8 thin slices good-quality white bread

Unsalted butter, at room temperature

Put the cucumber slices into a colander in the sink, sprinkle lightly with salt, and let stand for 20 minutes. Taste a slice to make sure you haven't added too much salt. If they are too salty, rinse the slices briefly under cool running water. Lay a few paper towels on a plate, arrange the cucumber slices in a single layer on the towels, and pat the slices dry.

Lay the bread slices on a work surface and spread each slice generously with softened butter. Arrange the cucumber slices, overlapping them, on 4 of the bread slices and sprinkle with pepper. Top with the remaining bread slices, buttered side down. Using a serrated knife, cut off the crusts from each sandwich, then cut each sandwich into 4 triangles and serve. Alternatively, use your favorite cookie cutters to cut out shapes from the bread (and snack on the scraps).

Variation

Avocado Tea Sandwiches: Replace the cucumber with 1 ripe avocado, pitted, peeled, and sliced. Sprinkle the avocado slices with salt and red pepper flakes instead of black pepper.

Ham & Cheese Tea Sandwiches

Mix and match your tea sandwich platter with these scrumptious bites and the classic Cucumber Tea Sandwiches on the opposite page. Not only will your party tray be colorful, but you'll also have something for everyone.

8 thin slices good-quality white bread

Dijon or honey mustard

8 thin slices Black Forest ham

8 thin slices Swiss cheese

Lay the bread slices on a work surface and spread each slice with a thin layer of mustard. Top 4 of the bread slices with the ham slices, dividing them evenly, then arrange the cheese slices over the ham. Top with the remaining 4 bread slices, mustard side down. Using a serrated knife, cut off the crusts from each sandwich, then cut each sandwich into 4 triangles and serve. Alternatively, use your favorite cookie cutters to cut out shapes from the bread (and snack on the scraps).

Make it fancy!

For an extra-special touch, use cookie cutters to cut your sandwiches into fun shapes! Try stars, hearts, crescent moons, flowers, or any molds you have on hand for an awe-inspiring snack.

Colorful Macarons

These delicate sandwich cookies take a little time and patience to prepare, but they're worth it. Choose your favorite color to tint the batter; you can also tint the filling with the same color or a different one, or keep it white. Cream of tartar is a powder that helps the egg whites whisk up nice and fluffy.

2 cups powdered sugar

1⅓ cups almond flour

3 large egg whites

1 teaspoon vanilla extract

½ teaspoon almond extract

¼ teaspoon cream of tartar

⅛ teaspoon salt

½ teaspoon pink or orange gel food coloring

White Chocolate Frosting (page 112)

Edible white glitter or pearl dust, for decorating (optional)

Line 2 cookie sheets with parchment paper. Use a 1½-inch round cookie cutter and a pen, trace 12 circles on each sheet of parchment. Turn the parchment over. The circle outlines will be visible through the paper.

Combine 1 cup of the powdered sugar and all the almond flour in a fine-mesh sieve. Set aside.

In a large bowl, using an electric mixer, beat together the egg whites, vanilla and almond extracts, cream of tartar, and salt on medium-high speed until foamy, about 30 seconds. Raise the speed to high and gradually beat in the remaining 1 cup powdered sugar, then continue beating until stiff, glossy peaks form, about 2 minutes longer.

Sift about one-third of the powdered sugar–almond flour mixture over the egg white mixture. Using a rubber spatula, fold it in gently just until blended. Repeat to fold in the remaining powdered sugar mixture in 2 batches. Add the food coloring and continue to fold the mixture just until the ingredients are fully combined and the batter flows in a thick, slow ribbon (about 40 strokes).

Spoon the batter into a piping bag fitted with a medium round tip (about ⅜ inch in diameter). Holding the piping bag so that the tip is about ½ inch above a circle outline on one of the parchment sheets, use the outline as a guide as you pipe the batter thickly onto each ~ *Continued on page 28* ~

Test for doneness
If the cookies seem done but still stick to the parchment, pop the macarons back into the oven for a few minutes longer.

~ *Continued from page 27* ~

circle, piping the outline first and then filling in the middle. Tap each cookie sheet firmly against the work surface two or three times to release any air bubbles in the batter. Let the cookies stand at room temperature until they look less wet and are a little tacky, 45 to 60 minutes.

Preheat the oven to 300°F. Bake, one sheet at a time, until the cookies have risen and set but not browned, about 20 minutes. The bottoms of the cookies should be dry and firm to the touch. Let the cookies cool on the cookie sheet on a wire rack for 1 minute, then transfer to the rack and let cool completely. Repeat to bake the remaining cookies.

While the cookies bake and cool, make the frosting.

Turn half of the cookies bottom side up. Spread about 1½ teaspoons of the frosting onto each cookie. Top with the remaining cookies, bottom side down, pressing the bases together gently.

Place the cookies in a single layer on a rimmed cookie sheet, cover with plastic wrap, and refrigerate for at least 1 day or up to 3 days, or freeze in an airtight container for up to 6 months. If freezing, once the macarons are frozen, stack them in an airtight container, then thaw in the refrigerator before serving. Just before serving, dust the tops with edible glitter, if using. Serve chilled or at cool room temperature.

No-Bake Cheesecake Flower Tarts

Use a flower-shaped cookie cutter and a mini muffin pan to create these adorable tiny treats. You'll need to allow time to refrigerate the tart dough before using it, but once it's baked, just fill the shells with an easy, no-bake cheesecake batter and top them with a dollop of jam.

Basic Tart Dough (page 116)

All-purpose flour, for dusting

Nonstick cooking spray

Prepare the tart dough and chill as directed.

Place the dough on a lightly floured work surface. Using a rolling pin, roll out the dough into a circle about ⅛ inch thick, lifting and rotating the dough a quarter turn after every pass or two and dusting the work surface with flour as needed to prevent sticking.

Preheat the oven to 375°F. Lightly spray every other cup of a 24-cup mini muffin pan (12 cups total) with cooking spray. (The crusts will be placed in every other cup so they are not touching.) Using a 4-inch flower-shaped cookie cutter, cut out as many flowers as possible. Carefully pull the dough scraps away from the cutouts, press them together, then roll them out and cut out more flowers. You should have 12 cutouts.

Transfer a flower cutout to a prepared muffin cup, pressing the center down into the bottom of the cup and folding the petals up and over the edge. Repeat with the remaining cutouts. Use a fork to prick the bottom and sides of the dough a few times. Bake until golden brown, about 20 minutes. Let the tart shells cool completely in the pan on a wire rack, then gently remove the shells from the pan and line them up on a work surface.

FOR THE FILLING

2 ounces cream cheese (4 tablespoons), at room temperature

2 tablespoons heavy cream

1 tablespoon powdered sugar

¼ teaspoon fresh lemon juice

¼ teaspoon vanilla extract

2–3 tablespoons jam, such as strawberry or raspberry, or marmalade

To make the filling, in a medium bowl, using an electric mixer, beat together the cream cheese, cream, powdered sugar, lemon juice, and vanilla on low speed until smooth and creamy, about 1 minute. Fit a piping bag with a medium round tip or use a large lock-top plastic bag with a corner snipped off. Using a spoon, scoop the cream cheese mixture into the piping bag. Holding the bag, pipe the cream cheese mixture into each tart shell, then smooth the top with your fingertip or an icing spatula. Each tart should be nearly full. Spoon about ½ teaspoon jam on top, gently spreading it to cover the cream cheese mixture. Arrange on a serving plate and serve right away or refrigerate for up to 1 day before serving.

Lemon Tartlets with Sugared Flowers

Did you know that some flowers are edible? They make super cool decorations for desserts—just be sure to choose blooms that are safe to eat (see the list below). Prepare the sugared flowers the day before you make the tartlets so they have time to dry.

FOR THE SUGARED FLOWERS

8–16 pesticide-free edible flowers, such as violet, pansy, culinary lavender, and/or rose petals

1 large egg white

Superfine sugar, for sprinkling

FOR THE LEMON CURD

1 large whole egg

4 large egg yolks

½ cup granulated sugar

⅓ cup fresh lemon juice, strained

2 tablespoons unsalted butter

12 store-bought mini tart shells, each about 1½ inches in diameter

To make the sugared flowers, gently wash the flowers under slowly running cool water and then set them on paper towels to dry, blotting them lightly with the towels if needed. The flowers must be fully dry before you begin. Line a rimmed cookie sheet with parchment paper. In a small bowl, whisk together the egg white and a few drops of water until foamy. Put the superfine sugar into a separate small bowl. Working with 1 flower at a time and using a small, clean paintbrush, lightly brush the egg white mixture over the front and back of the flower. Then, holding the flower over the sugar bowl, scoop up a little sugar and sprinkle it over the top, coating the flower completely. Set the flower aside on the prepared cookie sheet. Repeat with the remaining flowers. Let the flowers dry at room temperature for 12 to 24 hours until they are stiff and dry to the touch.

Meanwhile, to make the lemon curd, fill a saucepan about one-third full of water and bring to a gentle simmer over medium-low heat. Put the whole egg, egg yolks, granulated sugar, and lemon juice into a heatproof bowl that will rest snugly on the rim of the saucepan. Place the bowl on the saucepan over (but not touching) the simmering water. ~ Continued on page 34 ~

Tea party perfection

This yummy mochi treat is best served with a piping-hot cup of green tea.

~ **Continued from page 33** ~

Cook, stirring constantly with a wooden spoon or silicone spatula, until thickened, about 5 minutes. Remove from the heat, add the butter, and stir until melted and incorporated. Pour the curd through a fine-mesh sieve placed over a bowl, pressing against the curd with the back of the spoon or spatula to force as much through as possible. Cover the bowl with plastic wrap, pressing the plastic directly onto the surface of the curd (to prevent a "skin" from forming), and let cool until tepid. Refrigerate until chilled, about 1 hour, before using.

Line up the tartlet shells on a work surface. Fill each shell with about 1 tablespoon of the lemon curd, then garnish with the sugared blossoms. (You can use any leftover lemon curd as a topping for yogurt or ice cream.) Arrange the tarts on a large plate or tray and serve.

Hanami Dango

Hanami means "flower viewing" during cherry blossom season in Japan. Hanami dango are sweet dumplings made from two kinds of rice flour, colored to represent spring, and eaten on a skewer. Look for Mochiko sweetened rice flour at Asian grocery stores or online. You can use matcha powder or food coloring to make the green dumplings. Brush the dumplings with simple syrup after cooking for extra sweetness, if you like.

1 cup rice flour, plus more as needed

1 cup Mochiko sweetened rice flour, plus more as needed

¾ cup sugar

⅔ cup hot water

Green gel food coloring or 1 teaspoon matcha green tea powder

Red gel food coloring

Simple syrup, for serving (optional; see Note)

In a large bowl, whisk together both flours and the sugar. Very slowly drizzle in the hot water. Stir with a rubber spatula until all of the flour mixture is absorbed. The dough should be firm and slightly bouncy with a consistency similar to the texture of Play-Doh. If the dough is too sticky or wet, add more rice flour, 1 tablespoon of each flour at a time, until it is able to keep its shape when rolled into a ball. Let the dough rest 20 minutes

Divide the dough into 3 pieces and place each piece in a separate bowl. Add 1 to 2 drops of green food coloring or the matcha powder to the first bowl. Using your hands (wearing rubber gloves, if you like), knead the dough until all of the food coloring is absorbed. Add 1 to 2 drops of red food coloring to the second bowl. Using your hands (again wearing rubber gloves, if you like), knead the dough until all of the food coloring is absorbed. Leave the dough in the third bowl white.

Scoop out a teaspoon of dough and roll it into a ball between your palms. Set the ball aside on a large plate or cookie sheet and repeat with the remaining dough. You should have 12 balls in each color. ～ *Continued on page 37* ～

Simply sweet

To make simple syrup, in a small saucepan set over medium heat, combine ½ cup sugar with ½ cup water. Cook, stirring occasionally, until the sugar has dissolved. Remove from the heat and let cool.

~ *Continued from page 35* ~

Fill a large pot two-thirds full of water and bring to a boil over high heat. While the water comes to a boil, make an ice bath by filling a large bowl with ice and water, and set it next to the stovetop. Line a plate with paper towels and set it nearby.

Working in batches, if needed, carefully add the white balls to the boiling water, stirring immediately after adding each ball to the water so it doesn't stick to the bottom. Cook, stirring often so they don't stick together, until the dumplings start to float, about 8 minutes, then cook for 2 minutes longer. Using a slotted spoon, carefully transfer the dumplings to the ice bath and let cool for 1 minute. Then transfer the dumplings to the towel-lined plate. Repeat to cook and chill the pink balls and then the green balls. (Cooking them in this order will keep the water from discoloring.)

To assemble, place one pink, one white, and one green dumpling, in that order, onto a skewer. Brush with a simple syrup, if using. Repeats to assemble the remaining skewers. Arrange the skewers on a platter and serve.

Mini Victoria Sponge Cakes

"Sponge" is another way to say "cake" in Great Britain. You can bake these mini cakes in individual ceramic ramekins or in a special muffin pan that has removable bottoms.

FOR THE CAKE

1 cup (2 sticks) unsalted butter, at room temperature, plus more for greasing the ramekins

2 cups all-purpose flour, plus more for dusting the ramekins

1½ teaspoons baking powder

½ teaspoon salt

1 cup granulated sugar

4 large eggs, at room temperature

2 teaspoons vanilla extract

Whipped Cream (page 115)

⅔ cup strawberry or raspberry jam

Powdered sugar, for dusting

Preheat the oven to 350°F. Lightly butter and flour the bottom and sides of twelve ¾-cup straight-sided ramekins or a standard 12-cup muffin pan (ideally with removable bottoms). Have a large cookie sheet ready.

In a medium bowl, whisk together the flour, baking powder, and salt. In a large bowl, using an electric mixer, beat the butter on medium speed until smooth, about 1 minute. Add the granulated sugar, raise the speed to medium-high, and beat until fluffy and lighter in color, 2 to 3 minutes. Add the eggs, one at a time, beating well after each addition and adding the vanilla along with the final egg. On low speed, add the flour mixture and mix just until blended.

Divide the batter evenly among the prepared ramekins or muffin cups. Transfer the ramekins or muffin pan to the cookie sheet and bake until a wooden skewer inserted into the center of a cake comes out clean, 17 to 19 minutes. Transfer the cookie sheet to a wire rack and let the cakes cool for 15 minutes. Use an icing spatula to loosen the cake sides from the ramekins, then invert each ramekin onto a wire rack, lift it off, and turn the cake right side up. If using a muffin pan, loosen the cake sides the same way, then invert the pan onto a wire rack, lift off the pan, and turn the cakes right side up. (If the muffin cups have a removable bottom, push them up to release the cakes.) Let the cakes cool completely.

Using a serrated knife, cut the cakes in half horizontally. Arrange the bottom halves, cut side up, on a work surface. Spoon 1 tablespoon of the jam onto each cake bottom. Spread 1 tablespoon of the whipped cream on top of the jam. Arrange the tops, cut side down, on top of the cream. Dust the tops with powdered sugar and serve.

Cakes & Cupcakes

Rainbow Cupcakes

Sky blue and topped with mini marshmallow clouds and rainbow sour belts, these almost too-cute-to-eat cupcakes will get all the attention at your tea party. Bake them in patterned or metallic blue foil liners for an extra dose of color.

FOR THE CUPCAKES

2¾ cups cake flour

1 tablespoon
baking powder

½ teaspoon salt

1 cup (2 sticks)
unsalted butter,
at room temperature

1¾ cups sugar

4 large whole eggs

2 large egg yolks

2 teaspoons
vanilla extract

1 cup sour cream

8 drops of blue
food coloring

Fluffy Frosting
(page 115)

Rainbow sour belts,
for decorating

Miniature
marshmallows,
for decorating

Preheat the oven to 350°F. Line 2 standard 12-cup muffin pans with paper or foil liners.

In a medium bowl, whisk together the flour, baking powder, and salt. In a large bowl, using an electric mixer, beat together the butter and sugar on medium-high speed until light and fluffy, 2 to 3 minutes. Add the whole eggs and egg yolks one at a time, beating well after each addition. Turn off the mixer and scrape down the bowl. Add the vanilla and beat on medium-high speed until combined. Reduce the speed to low, add about half of the flour mixture, and mix just until blended. Add the sour cream and food coloring and beat just until combined. Add the remaining flour mixture and beat just until blended.

Divide the batter evenly among the prepared muffin cups. Bake the cupcakes until the tops are light golden brown and a wooden skewer inserted into the center of a cupcake comes out clean, 22 to 24 minutes. Let the cupcakes cool in the pans on wire racks for 10 minutes, then carefully transfer the cupcakes directly to the racks. Let cool completely, about 1 hour. While the cupcakes are cooling, make the frosting.

Using an icing spatula, spread the tops of the cupcakes with frosting. Cut the sour belts into twenty-four 2-inch lengths crosswise. Arc half of a sour belt like a rainbow and insert the ends into the frosting on each cupcake. Arrange marshmallows at the base of each arc to simulate clouds. Arrange the cupcakes on a large platter or tray and serve.

Strawberries & Cream Cupcakes

Give classic vanilla cupcakes a fruity, creamy makeover by adding some strawberry jam inside, then topping them with a swirl of irresistible cream cheese frosting and a fresh strawberry. These taste best during summer, when berries are in season.

FOR THE CUPCAKES

1¼ cups all-purpose flour

1¼ teaspoons
baking powder

¼ teaspoon salt

¾ cup sugar

6 tablespoons (¾ stick)
unsalted butter,
at room temperature

2 large eggs

1 teaspoon vanilla extract

⅓ cup whole milk

¼ cup strawberry jam
or preserves

Cream Cheese Frosting
(page 114)

12 strawberries

Preheat the oven to 350°F. Line a standard 12-cup muffin pan with paper or foil liners.

In a medium bowl, whisk together the flour, baking powder, and salt. In a large bowl, using an electric mixer, beat the sugar and butter on medium-high speed until light and fluffy, 2 to 3 minutes. Add the eggs, one at a time, beating well after each addition. Turn off the mixer and scrape down the bowl with a rubber spatula. Add the vanilla and beat until combined. Add about half of the flour mixture and mix on low speed just until blended. Add the milk and mix on low speed until combined. Add the remaining flour mixture and mix just until blended. Turn off the mixer, scrape down the bowl, and give the batter a final stir with the spatula.

Divide the batter evenly among the prepared muffin cups. Drop 1 teaspoon jam onto the center of each (the jam will sink into the batter during baking). Bake until the tops are light golden brown and a wooden skewer inserted into the center of a cupcake comes out with only a few crumbs and some jam attached, 18 to 20 minutes. Let the cupcakes cool in the pan on a wire rack for 10 minutes, then carefully transfer the cupcakes directly to the rack. Let cool completely, about 1 hour. While the cupcakes cool, make the frosting.

Using a small icing spatula or a butter knife, or a piping bag fitted with a large round tip, top the cupcakes with frosting and place a strawberry in the center.

Butterfly Cupcakes

For these fancy-looking treats, the cupcake tops are sliced off, cut in half, and perched in the frosting topping to resemble butterfly wings. They're the perfect addition to a nature-inspired outdoor garden party. Use colorful paper liners to make them even more festive.

FOR THE CUPCAKES

1⅔ cups all-purpose flour

1¼ teaspoons baking powder

½ teaspoon salt

½ cup (1 stick) unsalted butter, at room temperature

¾ cup granulated sugar

2 large eggs, at room temperature

½ teaspoon vanilla extract

½ cup whole milk

Fluffy Frosting (page 115)

Strawberry or raspberry jam

 Preheat the oven to 350°F. Line a standard 12-cup muffin pan with paper or foil liners.

In a small bowl, whisk together the flour, baking powder, and salt. In a large bowl, using an electric mixer, beat the butter on medium speed until smooth, about 1 minute. Add the sugar, raise the speed to medium-high, and beat until fluffy and lighter in color, 2 to 3 minutes. Add 1 egg, beat well, and add the vanilla with the second egg. On low speed, add about half of the flour mixture and mix just until blended, then add the milk and mix until blended. Add the remaining flour mixture and mix just until blended.

Divide the batter evenly among the prepared muffin cups and smooth it with an icing spatula. Bake until the tops are light golden brown and a wooden skewer inserted into the center of a cupcake comes out clean, 17 to 19 minutes. Let the cupcakes cool in the pan on a wire rack for 15 minutes. Lift the cupcakes from the pan and arrange, top side up, on the rack. Let cool completely. While the cupcakes are cooling, make the frosting.

Using a serrated knife, cut off the domed top from each cupcake and cut it in half to form the butterfly "wings". Using an icing spatula, spread the tops of the cupcakes with frosting. Put a small dollop (about ¼ teaspoon) of the jam in the center of the frosting. Gently push 2 wings, cut side down and at a slight angle, into the frosting, positioning them on either side of the jam. Serve right away.

Gluten-Free Nutty Tea Cakes

The combination of almond flour, rice flour, and pistachios makes these two-bite gluten-free cakes super light—they have a more tender texture than cupcakes made with all-purpose flour. Decorate them with a dusting of powdered sugar and some pretty sugared flowers, if you like.

Nonstick cooking spray

½ cup almond flour

½ cup toasted unsalted pistachios

⅓ cup granulated sugar

¼ cup white rice flour

1 teaspoon baking powder

¼ teaspoon salt

3 large egg whites

½ cup (1 stick) unsalted butter, melted and cooled

Powdered sugar, for dusting

Sugared Flowers (page 33) or fresh raspberries, for decorating (optional)

Preheat the oven to 350°F. Spray a 24-cup mini muffin pan with cooking spray.

In a food processor, combine the almond flour, pistachios, granulated sugar, rice flour, baking powder, and salt and process until very finely ground, about 2 minutes. Transfer to a bowl.

Add the egg whites to the flour mixture and whisk until well combined. Add the butter in three additions, whisking well after each addition.

Spoon the batter into the prepared muffin cups, dividing it evenly and filling the cups nearly to the rims. Let the batter sit for 10 minutes. Bake the cakes until light golden brown around the edges, about 15 minutes. Let cool in the muffin pan on a wire rack for 5 minutes, then carefully transfer the cupcakes directly to the rack. Let cool completely.

Arrange the cakes on a large plate and, using a fine-mesh sieve, dust them with powdered sugar. If you like, decorate each cake with a sugared flower or raspberry before serving.

Iced Lemon Drizzle Cupcakes

Bake these double-lemon cupcakes (there's lemon in both the cake and the glaze) in colorful cupcake liners that match your party's theme, and adorn them with colorful sprinkles Adding sour cream to the batter keeps it moist. Be sure to zest the lemon before you juice it.

FOR THE CUPCAKES

1¼ cups all-purpose flour

½ teaspoon
baking powder

½ teaspoon baking soda

¼ teaspoon salt

4 tablespoons (½ stick)
unsalted butter,
at room temperature

¾ cup granulated sugar

2 teaspoons grated
lemon zest

1 large egg

¾ cup sour cream

FOR THE GLAZE

1 cup powdered sugar

2 tablespoons fresh
lemon juice, plus more
if needed

Metallic sprinkles,
for decorating (optional)

 Preheat the oven to 325°F. Line a standard 12-cup muffin pan with paper or foil liners.

To make the cupcakes, in a medium bowl, whisk together the flour, baking powder, baking soda, and salt. In a large bowl, using an electric mixer, beat together the butter, granulated sugar, and lemon zest on medium speed until fluffy and pale, about 3 minutes. Add the egg and beat until combined. Turn off the mixer and scrape down the bowl with a rubber spatula. Add half of the flour mixture and beat on low speed just until combined. Then add the sour cream and beat just until combined. Add the remaining flour mixture and beat just until combined. Turn off the mixer, scrape down the bowl, and give the batter a final stir.

Divide the batter evenly among the prepared muffin cups, filling them about three-fourths full. Bake the cupcakes until golden brown and a wooden skewer inserted into the center of a cupcake comes out clean, 18 to 20 minutes. Let the cupcakes cool in the muffin pan on a wire rack for 10 minutes, then carefully transfer the cupcakes directly to the rack. Let cool completely.

To make the glaze, in a small bowl, whisk together the powdered sugar and lemon juice until smooth and spreadable, adding more lemon juice, if needed, until the glaze is thick but pourable. Spoon some of the glaze on top of each cooled cupcake and, using the back of the spoon, spread it to the edge. Decorate with sprinkles, if you like. Let the glaze stand for 1 to 2 minutes until it sets, then serve.

Touch of green
If you'd like, substitute a vibrant garnish of fresh mint leaves for the sprinkles or sanding sugar.

Mini Chocolate-Mint Cupcakes

These tiny treats taste just like peppermint hot chocolate in cupcake form. Their brownie-like texture gets a flavor kick from peppermint extract in the batter and in the fluffy frosting.

4 ounces bittersweet chocolate, chopped

4 tablespoons (½ stick) unsalted butter, cut into pieces

¾ cup sugar

2 large eggs

½ teaspoon vanilla extract

¼ teaspoon peppermint extract

¼ teaspoon salt

¼ cup plus 2 tablespoons all-purpose flour

Fluffy Mint Frosting (page 115)

Sprinkles or sanding sugar, for decorating (optional)

Preheat the oven to 350°F. Line a 24-cup mini muffin pan with paper or foil liners.

In a medium microwave-safe bowl, combine the chocolate and butter. Microwave on high power, stirring every 20 seconds, just until the mixture is melted and smooth. Let cool completely.

Add the sugar to the chocolate mixture and stir with a whisk until blended. Whisk in the eggs, one at a time, mixing until well combined after each addition. Whisk in the vanilla and peppermint extracts, and the salt. Add the flour and fold gently with a rubber spatula just until no white streaks remain; do not overmix.

Divide the batter evenly among the prepared muffin cups. Bake until the tops are crackly and a wooden skewer inserted into the center of a cupcake comes out with only a few crumbs attached, 18 to 20 minutes. Let the cupcakes cool in the pan on a wire rack for 10 minutes, then carefully transfer the cupcakes directly to the rack. Let cool completely, about 1 hour.

Using a small icing spatula or a butter knife, or a piping bag fitted with a star tip, top the cupcakes with the frosting, then decorate with sprinkles, if using.

Molten Chocolate Cupcakes

There's a surprise inside these super-chocolaty cupcakes: more chocolate! Adding a piece of bittersweet chocolate halfway through baking makes them gooey.

Nonstick cooking spray

3½ ounces semisweet chocolate, chopped

4 tablespoons (½ stick) unsalted butter, cut into 4 pieces

3 large eggs, separated, at room temperature

2 tablespoons all-purpose flour

Pinch of salt

¼ cup sugar

1 (4-ounce) bittersweet chocolate bar, broken evenly into 12 pieces

Preheat the oven to 375°F. Lightly spray a standard 12-cup muffin pan with cooking spray.

In a medium microwave-safe bowl, combine the chocolate and butter. Microwave on low power for 1 minute. Stir and continue to microwave, stirring every 20 seconds, just until the mixture is melted and smooth. Set aside to cool slightly.

Whisk the egg yolks into the chocolate mixture until well combined, about 30 seconds. Add the flour and whisk until combined.

In a medium bowl, using an electric mixer, beat the egg whites and salt on medium-high speed until foamy. Slowly add the sugar, beating continuously, until soft peaks form (and tips bend slightly when a beater is lifted). Using a whisk, gently fold a third of the egg white mixture into the chocolate mixture to lighten it. Fold in the egg white mixture in 2 more additions until no white streaks remain.

Divide the batter evenly among the prepared muffin cups, filling them about two-thirds full. Bake the cupcakes for 5 minutes and then remove the pan from the oven. Working quickly, insert one piece of bittersweet chocolate into the center of each cupcake. Return the pan to the oven and bake until the cupcakes have risen and turned brown around the edges, 3 to 5 minutes more.

Let the cupcakes cool slightly in the pan on a wire rack, about 5 minutes. Use a small offset spatula to transfer the cupcakes to plates. Serve right away.

Orange Upside-Down Cakes

Thin orange slices caramelize in butter and brown sugar to create these fancy fruit-topped treats. A small icing spatula helps release the cakes and unstick any orange slices.

6 tablespoons (¾ stick) unsalted butter, melted and cooled, plus ½ cup (1 stick), and more for greasing, at room temperature

2 oranges (1 zested, 1 cut into 6 very thin slices)

¾ cup firmly packed light brown sugar

1 cup all-purpose flour

1 teaspoon baking powder

½ teaspoon baking soda

¼ teaspoon salt

½ cup granulated sugar

2 large eggs, at room temperature

¼ cup heavy cream, at room temperature

1 teaspoon vanilla extract

Preheat the oven to 350°F. Lightly butter six 1-cup ramekins.

Sprinkle 2 tablespoons of the brown sugar into each prepared ramekin. Add 1 tablespoon of the melted butter, evenly covering the sugar. Place 1 orange slice in each ramekin. Place the ramekins on a rimmed cookie sheet.

In a small bowl, whisk together the flour, baking powder, baking soda, and salt. In a large bowl, using an electric mixer, beat the remaining ½ cup butter on medium speed until smooth, about 1 minute. Raise the speed to medium-high, add the granulated sugar and orange zest, and beat until fluffy and lighter in color, 3 to 5 minutes. Add the eggs, one at a time, beating well after each addition. Using a rubber spatula, fold in the flour mixture until well blended. Add the cream and vanilla and stir until thoroughly incorporated.

Divide the batter evenly among the prepared ramekins, spooning it over the orange slices. Bake the cakes until the tops are golden brown and a wooden skewer inserted into the center of a cake comes out clean, about 35 minutes. Let the ramekins cool on the pan on a wire rack for 10 minutes.

Run an icing spatula around the edge of each ramekin to loosen the cake sides. Working with 1 cake at a time, invert a small plate over the ramekin, then invert the ramekin and plate together in a single quick motion. Tap the bottom of the ramekin with the spatula handle to loosen the cake, then lift off the ramekin.

Fruity Desserts

Pink-Orange Tartlets

When the ruby-red juice of blood oranges is mixed with a creamy custard, it creates a beautiful pink color. You can substitute the same amount of juice from Cara Cara oranges and reduce the sugar to ⅔ cup. You'll need small tartlet pans, preferably with removable bottoms.

Cream Cheese Tart Dough (page 116)

2 large whole eggs, plus 3 large egg yolks

½ cup fresh blood orange or Cara Cara orange juice, strained

2 tablespoons fresh lemon juice, strained

¾ cup granulated sugar

½ cup (1 stick) unsalted butter, cut into pieces

2 teaspoons grated blood orange or Cara Cara orange zest

Powdered sugar, for dusting

Blood orange or Cara Cara orange slices, peeled, for decorating (optional)

Prepare the dough as directed. Cut the dough into 6 equal portions, and place one portion in each of six 4-inch tartlet pans. Press the dough evenly over the bottom and up the sides of each pan until it is even with the rim. Trim any overhang. Freeze until the dough is firm, about 30 minutes.

Preheat the oven to 400°F. Line the tartlets with foil and fill with pie weights or dried beans. Place on a rimmed cookie sheet and bake until the crusts start to look dry, about 15 minutes. Remove the weights and foil. Reduce the oven temperature to 350°F and continue to bake until the crusts are lightly browned, about 5 minutes. Let cool on the cookie sheet.

Reduce the oven temperature to 325°F. In the top of a double boiler over (but not touching) barely simmering water, whisk together the whole eggs, egg yolks, orange juice, lemon juice, and granulated sugar. Whisk constantly until the mixture is thick enough to coat the back of a spoon and registers 160°F on an instant-read thermometer, about 12 minutes. Remove the mixture from over the water and pour it through a medium-mesh sieve into a bowl. Add the butter and orange zest and stir until the butter melts and is mixed in well. Let stand for 10 minutes, then spoon the mixture into the cooled tartlet shells.

Bake the tartlets until the centers are set, 12 to 15 minutes. Let the tartlets cool on the cookie sheet on a wire rack for 20 minutes. Cover and refrigerate for at least 3 hours or up to overnight. The filling will thicken further. To serve, unmold each tartlet, dust lightly with powdered sugar, and decorate with orange slices, if using.

Fresh Lemon Mousse Parfaits

Top these creamy, bright yellow custards with your favorite berry—raspberries, blueberries, or blackberries will all look and taste delicious. Remember to leave enough time to let the mousse set in the refrigerator, 2 to 3 hours, and to take the parfaits out of the fridge 20 minutes before you serve them.

1 packages (2¼ teaspoons) unflavored powdered gelatin

1 cup granulated sugar

⅛ teaspoon salt

2 teaspoons finely grated lemon zest

⅔ cup fresh lemon juice (about 8 lemons)

4 large egg yolks

2 cups heavy cream

¼ cup powdered sugar

1 pint (8 ounces) raspberries, blueberries, or blackberries

Whipped Cream (page 115)

 Make an ice bath by filling a large bowl with ice and 2 cups water. Set aside.

Pour ¼ cup water into a medium saucepan and sprinkle with the gelatin. Let stand until the gelatin softens and swells, 5 to 10 minutes. Stir in the granulated sugar, salt, lemon zest and juice, and egg yolks. Set the pan over medium heat and cook, stirring constantly, until the mixture thickens and the gelatin dissolves completely, 6 to 8 minutes. (Be careful not to let it boil.) Remove from the heat and set the saucepan in the ice bath until the mixture is cool to the touch. Remove the pan from the ice bath and let sit at room temperature.

In a large bowl, using an electric mixer, beat the cream and powdered sugar on medium speed until soft peaks form, 4 to 6 minutes. Using a rubber spatula, fold in the lemon mixture until smooth. Spoon the mousse into 6 to 8 glass jars, filling each two-thirds full. Refrigerate the mousse until chilled, 2 to 3 hours.

Remove from the refrigerator about 20 minutes before serving. Top each parfait with a handful of berries and a dollop of whipped cream. Serve right away.

Raspberry-Chocolate Tartlets

This delicious chocolate tart dough bakes in muffin cups—no extra baking gear required! It chills in the refrigerator twice for 30 minutes each pop, so leave enough time when preparing these fruity treats with a no-bake raspberry filling.

FOR THE DOUGH

½ cup (1 stick) unsalted butter, at cool room temperature, cut into pieces

⅓ cup powdered sugar

1 large egg yolk

1 teaspoon vanilla extract

¼ teaspoon salt

1¼ cups all-purpose flour, plus more for dusting

¼ cup unsweetened cocoa powder

Nonstick cooking spray

FOR THE FILLING

1 cup heavy cream

2 tablespoons seedless raspberry jam

12 fresh raspberries, for garnish

To make the dough, in a large bowl, using an electric mixer, beat together the butter, powdered sugar, egg yolk, vanilla, and salt on medium-low speed until smooth and creamy, about 1 minute. Turn off the mixer and scrape down the bowl with a rubber spatula. Sift together the flour and cocoa powder over the butter mixture and beat on low speed just until the mixture is evenly moistened and starts to clump together, about 1 minute. Dump the dough onto a clean work surface and press it into a thick disk. Wrap the disk in plastic wrap and refrigerate for at least 30 minutes or up to overnight.

Lightly spray a standard 12-cup muffin pan with cooking spray. On a lightly floured work surface, using a rolling pin, roll out the dough into a round about ⅛ inch thick. If the dough tears, press it back together. Using a 3-inch fluted cookie cutter, cut out as many rounds as possible. Gather up the scraps, press them together, roll out, and cut out more rounds as needed to make a total of 12 rounds. Transfer each round to a prepared muffin cup, gently pressing it evenly onto the bottom and partly up the sides. Place the lined muffin cups in the freezer to firm up for 30 minutes before baking. ~ *Continued on page 62* ~

Top it off

If you don't have ripe or in-season raspberries for the garnish, swap in banana slices or a small circle of blueberries.

~ Continued from page 60 ~

Preheat the oven to 350°F. Bake the tartlet shells until cooked through, about 15 minutes.

Let the tartlet shells cool in the muffin pan on a wire rack for 10 minutes, then carefully remove the tartlet shells from the muffin cups and let cool completely on the rack.

When the shells are cool, make the filling. In a bowl, using an electric mixer, beat together the cream and raspberry jam on medium-high speed until stiff peaks form, about 5 minutes. The peaks should stand straight when the beaters are lifted. Be careful not to overwhip.

Spoon the filling into a piping bag fitted with a large star tip, or use a large lock-top plastic bag with a corner snipped off. Pipe the filling into the tartlet shells, dividing it evenly. Top each tartlet with a raspberry. Serve right away.

Summer Fruit Buttermilk Tart

Prebaking the crust for this tart using pie weights or dried beans will prevent it from puffing up in the oven while the tart is baking. Be sure to pay close attention to the buttermilk custard on the stove, whisking it constantly so it doesn't clump or bubble over. Top the finished tart with a rainbow of fresh summer fruits.

Basic Tart Dough (page 116)

All-purpose flour, for dusting

1½ cups buttermilk

½ cup heavy cream

2 teaspoons fresh lemon juice (about ½ lemon)

1 cup sugar

1½ tablespoons cornstarch

Pinch of salt

2 large egg yolks

1 tablespoon unsalted butter, at room temperature

Fresh mixed fruit, such as raspberries, blueberries, or blackberries, hulled and sliced strawberries, nectarine slices, plum slices, or kiwi slices, for decorating

Prepare the dough and chill as directed. Have ready a 9-inch round tart pan. On a lightly floured work surface, using a rolling pin, roll out the dough into a 12-inch round about ¼ inch thick. Carefully fold the dough in half to make a half-moon shape and transfer it to the tart pan. Unfold the dough and gently press it into the bottom and up the sides of the pan, letting it hang slightly over the edges. Using your fingers, gently press down all around the top edge of the pan to remove excess dough. Freeze the dough until firm, about 30 minutes.

While the dough is freezing, preheat the oven to 375°F. Remove the tart pan from the freezer, line it with parchment paper, and fill with pie weights or dried beans. Place the tart pan on a rimmed cookie sheet and bake until the crust dries out, about 15 minutes. Remove the weights and parchment and let the crust cool while you make the filling.

In a medium saucepan, combine the buttermilk, cream, and lemon juice. In a small bowl, whisk together the 1 cup sugar, cornstarch, and salt. Add to the saucepan along with the egg yolks and whisk to blend. ～ *Continued on page 65* ～

Summer's bounty

No berries? Any ripe summer fruit will bring out the best of this lemon-kissed treat. Try sliced nectarines or apricots, or halved pitted cherries.

~ *Continued from page 63* ~

Set the saucepan over medium heat and cook, whisking constantly, until the mixture reaches a simmer and is as thick as pudding, about 6 minutes. Strain through a fine-mesh sieve into a large liquid measuring cup, using a rubber spatula to help push the mixture through the sieve and off the bottom. Whisk in the butter until blended. Pour the filling into the cooled tart shell.

Bake until the filling looks dry but jiggles slightly when the pan is shaken, 14 to 16 minutes. Let the tart cool in the pan for about 5 minutes, then transfer to a wire rack and let cool completely.

Individual Cherry Cobblers

Although they look super fancy and impressive, these fruity treats are easy to make. Bake the fruit mixture for a few minutes first to help it set, then add the biscuit-like topping and continue baking until golden brown and scrumptious.

FOR THE FILLING

3 pounds fresh sweet cherries, pitted

1 tablespoon fresh lemon juice

3 tablespoons sugar

FOR THE TOPPING

⅔ cup buttermilk

1 teaspoon vanilla extract

1½ cups all-purpose flour

⅓ cup plus 1 tablespoon sugar

1 teaspoon baking powder

½ teaspoon baking soda

½ teaspoon salt

¾ teaspoon ground cinnamon

6 tablespoons (¾ stick) cold unsalted butter, cut into ½-inch pieces

Vanilla ice cream, for serving (optional)

Preheat the oven to 375°F. Place six 1-cup ramekins on a rimmed cookie sheet.

To make the filling, in a large bowl, stir together the cherries, lemon juice, and the 3 tablespoons sugar until well mixed. Divide the fruit mixture among the ramekins and bake for 10 minutes.

To make the topping, in a small bowl, stir together the buttermilk and vanilla; set aside. In a large bowl, whisk together the flour, ⅓ cup of the sugar, baking powder, baking soda, salt, and ½ teaspoon of the cinnamon. Add the butter and, using a pastry blender or 2 knives, cut it into the flour mixture until the mixture forms large coarse crumbs the size of small peas. Pour the buttermilk mixture over the flour mixture and, using a large wooden spoon, stir just until combined and a soft, sticky, evenly moistened dough forms.

Drop the dough by heaping spoonfuls onto the hot fruit, spacing it evenly over the surface in each ramekin. (You can use an ice cream scoop for this step.) The topping will not cover the fruit, but it will spread during baking. In a small bowl, stir together the remaining 1 tablespoon sugar and ¼ teaspoon cinnamon. Sprinkle over the dough.

Bake until the fruit filling is bubbling, the topping is browned, and a wooden skewer inserted into the topping comes out clean, 30 to 35 minutes. Let cool on a wire rack for 15 minutes. Serve warm with a scoop of ice cream on top, if you like.

Little Apple Galettes

Use a mix of firm red and pink apples so their different-colored skins create an ombré effect. To make a circle template, trace a bowl that is about 6 inches in diameter and trace around it on a piece of cardboard.

Basic Pie Dough (page 117)

All-purpose flour, for dusting

½ cup sugar

2 tablespoons cornstarch

¼ teaspoon ground cinnamon

⅛ teaspoon salt

2 pounds apples, cored, quartered, and sliced about ⅛ inch thick

1 tablespoon fresh lemon juice

1 large egg

1 tablespoon heavy cream

Turbinado or raw sugar, for sprinkling (optional)

Prepare and chill the dough as directed. Line 2 cookie sheets with parchment paper.

On a lightly floured work surface, cut the dough in half. Use a rolling pin to roll out both halves into rounds about ⅛ inch thick. (It's easier to work with two smaller pieces of dough than one very large one.) Using a 6-inch cardboard circle and a small, sharp knife, cut out 2 or 3 circles from each dough round. Press the scraps together and reroll them to cut out more circles. You should have a total of 8 circles (4 circles from each dough round).

Place the dough circles on the prepared cookie sheets.

In a small bowl, stir together the sugar, cornstarch, cinnamon, and salt. In a large bowl, combine the apples and lemon juice and toss well to coat. Add the sugar mixture to the bowl with the apple slices and toss the apple slices until evenly coated. ～ Continued on page 68 ～

Make it pretty

To create an ombré effect, organize the apples by the color of their skins and arrange them in a row from dark to light inside the pie dough.

~ *Continued from page 67* ~

Arrange about ½ cup of the apple slices in a neat row in the center of each dough circle, leaving a 1-inch border all around. Fold the border up and over the filling of each galette, forming tight pleats all around the edges and leaving the centers open. Refrigerate the galettes on the cookie sheets until the dough is firm, 20 to 30 minutes.

While the galettes are chilling, preheat the oven to 375°F. In a small bowl, beat the egg and cream together with a fork or whisk. Remove the galettes from the refrigerator and lightly brush the crust with the egg mixture (you will not use all of it). Sprinkle the crust with turbinado or granulated sugar, if using.

Bake the galettes until the crusts are golden and the juice around the apples has thickened, 30 to 40 minutes. Let cool on the cookie sheets on a wire rack for about 15 minutes before serving.

Blueberry Hand Pies

The key to making pie dough is ensuring the butter is very cold so that it doesn't melt when baked. It's a snap to make piecrust in a food processor. If you don't have one, or want to save a little time, you can use two sheets of store-bought refrigerated piecrust.

Basic Pie Dough (page 117)

All-purpose flour, for dusting

1 pint (8 ounces) blueberries

3 tablespoons granulated sugar

2 tablespoons cornstarch

Pinch of salt

1 large egg

1 tablespoon heavy cream

Turbinado or raw sugar, for sprinkling

Prepare the dough and chill as directed. Transfer the dough to a lightly floured work surface and divide it in half. Using a rolling pin, roll each half into a round at least 12 inches in diameter and about ⅛ inch thick. Using a 4-inch round cutter, cut out 3 or 4 circles from each dough round. Press the scraps together, roll them out, and cut out more circles. You should have a total of 12 circles.

Line a cookie sheet with parchment paper. In a medium bowl, toss together the blueberries, granulated sugar, cornstarch, and salt. Lay 6 dough rounds on the prepared cookie sheet, spacing them evenly. Divide the blueberries evenly among the dough rounds. Using a small pastry brush, dampen the edge of each round with cold water. Lay the remaining dough rounds over the blueberries. Gently press the top of each dough round down over the berries; the edges of the dough rounds will not line up. Using the tines of a fork, press the outer edge of the dough rounds together. Refrigerate until the dough is firm, 15 to 20 minutes.

Preheat the oven to 375°F.

In a small bowl, beat the egg and cream together with a fork or whisk. Lightly brush the dough rounds with the egg mixture (you will not use all of it). Sprinkle each round with turbinado sugar.

Bake the pies until golden brown, 35 to 40 minutes. Let the pies cool slightly on the cookie sheet on a wire rack. Serve warm.

Apricot Puff-Pastry Twists

Super-flaky puff pastry is made up of lots of alternating layers of paper-thin dough and butter. For these adorable treats, cut store-bought pastry into strips and twist them. A pastry brush is a helpful tool.

1 sheet store-bought frozen puff pastry (about ½ pound), thawed overnight in the refrigerator

All-purpose flour, for dusting

¼ cup apricot jam

1 large egg white

1 tablespoon turbinado or granulated sugar

 Line a cookie sheet with parchment paper.

Place the puff pastry on a lightly floured work surface. Carefully unfold it and press it flat. Using a pizza cutter or sharp knife, cut the sheet in half to make 2 rectangles. Using a pastry brush, evenly brush 1 rectangle with the jam. Place the other rectangle on top of the jam-covered rectangle, lining up the edges and gently pressing them together. Put the egg white in a small bowl and beat it lightly with a fork. Using the pastry brush, lightly brush the top of the pastry with some of the egg white. Sprinkle half of the sugar evenly over the top, pressing it in gently so it adheres. Carefully turn the pastry over, brush the top side with the egg white, sprinkle with the remaining sugar, and again press so that the sugar adheres.

Using the pizza cutter or knife, cut the pastry rectangle lengthwise into 6 equal strips. Twist the ends of each strip in opposite directions to give the strip a spiraled look, then transfer the twists to the prepared cookie sheet, spacing them about 1½ inches apart. Refrigerate for 20 minutes.

While the twists are chilling, preheat the oven to 400°F.

Bake the pastry twists until they are golden brown and the jam is bubbling, about 15 minutes. Turn off the oven and leave the twists in the oven for 5 minutes longer to crisp. Transfer the twists to a wire rack to cool briefly, then serve warm.

Dim Sum Mango Pancakes

Many Asian countries have a custom of eating small servings of food, called dim sum. In a restaurant, the dim sum are delivered to the table from a rolling cart. This sweet addition to the dim sum cart was likely developed in Australia, but the combination of an eggy, crepe-like pancake filled with ripe mango and cold whipped cream is delicious anywhere in the world.

⅔ cup all-purpose flour

½ teaspoon salt

4 large eggs

3 tablespoons sugar

⅔ cup whole milk

1 teaspoon vanilla extract

3 tablespoons canola or vegetable oil, plus more for greasing the pan

1 large ripe mango

Whipped Cream (page 115)

In a small bowl, whisk together the flour and salt. In a large bowl, whisk together the eggs, sugar, and milk until well blended. Slowly add the flour mixture and whisk until no lumps remain. Add the vanilla and 3 tablespoons oil and mix until smooth. Let rest at room temperature for 30 minutes.

Using a paper towel, coat a medium nonstick skillet or crepe pan very lightly with oil and set the pan over low heat. Have a plate and a kitchen towel nearby. Transfer the batter to a measuring pitcher for easy pouring, if desired. Pour about ¼ cup batter into the center of the pan and gently swirl the pan so the batter spreads and coats the surface in an even circle. Cover the pan and cook until the pancake has set, 1 to 1½ minutes (the pancake should only brown lightly, if at all, on the bottom). Using an icing spatula, carefully lift the edges of the pancake from the pan, then slide the spatula underneath the pancake to release it from the pan. Transfer the pancake to a plate, cover it with a kitchen towel, and repeat to cook the remaining batter. You should have 8 pancakes. Cover the plate of pancakes with plastic wrap and refrigerate for 30 minutes. ~ Continued on page 74 ~

Chill for flavor

For the best flavor and texture, keep all ingredients cold and allow enough time for chilling at each step.

~ *Continued from page 73* ~

While the pancakes are cooling, prepare the mango. Stand the mango upright on a cutting board and carefully cut off the rounded sides away from the pit, then cut off the smaller round ends. Using a large spoon, scoop the mango flesh out of the peel. Slice the flesh into sticks about 1 inch wide. Place the mango sticks on a plate and freeze until ready to use.

Prepare the whipped cream as directed. Cover the bowl with plastic wrap and refrigerate until ready to use.

To assemble the pancakes, place 1 pancake, browned side up, on a clean work surface. Place 2 cold mango slices in the center of the bottom third of the pancake and top with 1 tablespoon of whipped cream. Starting with the edge nearest you, roll the pancake up like a burrito, tucking the sides in tightly as you roll. Place the pancake, seam side down, on a plate. Repeat to roll the remaining pancakes. (You will not use all of the whipped cream; save for another use.) Refrigerate the rolled pancakes for at least 15 minutes or up to 4 hours. Cut each pancake in half and serve cold.

Colorful Fruit Jellies

For these sparkly and super-chewy candies, match the food coloring to the flavor of the fruit extract—use red for raspberry and orange for orange jellies. These party-perfect jellies are also great gifts and last for 2 weeks.

Nonstick cooking spray

1 cup light corn syrup

2 cups sugar

1 (4-ounce) package powdered fruit pectin

¼ teaspoon baking soda

1½ teaspoons raspberry or orange extract

5 drops red or orange food coloring

Spray the bottom and sides of an 8-inch square baking pan with cooking spray. Cut an 8-by-12-inch piece of parchment paper. Line the pan with the parchment paper, covering the bottom and overhanging two sides. Spray the parchment with cooking spray.

In a saucepan over low heat, combine the corn syrup and 1 cup of the sugar. Heat, stirring often, until the sugar has dissolved, about 5 minutes. Raise the heat to medium-high and bring to a low boil, stirring occasionally. Meanwhile, in another saucepan over medium heat, combine the pectin, baking soda, and ¾ cup water and bring to a low boil, stirring occasionally.

Remove both saucepans from the heat. Carefully pour the pectin mixture into the corn syrup mixture and stir to mix. Add the raspberry extract and red food coloring and stir until blended. Immediately pour the jelly mixture into the prepared baking pan. Let stand until set, at least 1 hour or overnight.

Holding the ends of the parchment, lift the jelly sheet onto a cutting board. Using a large, sharp knife, cut the sheet into 8 rows, give the pan a quarter turn, and cut into 8 rows again to make sixty-four 1-inch pieces. Pour the remaining 1 cup sugar onto a plate. Working with 1 row at a time, toss the jellies in the sugar until evenly coated. Store in an airtight container at room temperature for up to 2 weeks.

Watermelon "Layer" Cake

Layers of sweet watermelon held together with skewers and decorated with fresh berries create a showstopping cake at a summer garden party. Ask an adult to help you cut the watermelon since you'll need a large, sharp knife to create the cylindrical layers.

1 large seedless watermelon

1 cup berries, such as blueberries or blackberries

Fresh fruit slices, such as apple, mango, or kiwi

Fresh mint leaves for garnish

Ask an adult to help you cut the watermelon. Using a large knife, cut off the ends of the watermelon and discard them, then cut the watermelon crosswise into 2 or 3 pieces of equal thickness. Place the largest piece, cut side down, on a cutting board; set the other pieces aside. Find a plate or a bowl that is slightly smaller than the circumference of the watermelon. Turn the plate upside down on the large piece of watermelon and trace along its edge with the tip of a knife to make a perfect circle. Remove the plate and, using a sharp knife (ask an adult for help), cut along the traced edge to remove the rind and form a cylinder shape.

Place the cylinder, cut side down, on a rimmed cake plate to make the bottom "cake" layer and insert wooden skewers or chopsticks into the center, leaving 2 inches of each skewer exposed.

Repeat the cutting process with the other watermelon pieces, using more plates as needed, each one about 2 inches smaller in width than the one used before it. Place the middle watermelon layer over the bottom layer, centering it and pressing it onto the skewers. Insert 2 wooden skewers or chopsticks into the center of the middle layer, leaving 2 inches of each skewer exposed. Place the smallest watermelon layer on top, centering it and pressing it gently onto the skewers. Save any remaining watermelon for another use.

Arrange the berries on top. Decorate the sides with fruit slices. Garnish with mint leaves. To serve, remove the skewers and cut the watermelon cake into pieces and serve.

Savory Snacks

Garden Flower Sandwich Cake

Inspired by classic finger sandwiches with layers of flatbread, cream cheese, cucumbers, and smoked salmon, this is the perfect "cake" for an alfresco tea party when decorated with oodles of edible flowers. Be sure to use pesticide-free edible flowers, available at farmers' markets and in the produce section of many grocery stores.

5 flat gyro pita wraps or thick, soft white pita bread, each 6½ to 7 inches in diameter and ¼ inch thick

2 (8-ounce) containers whipped cream cheese

¼ cup plus ⅓ cup fromage blanc (or fresh farmer cheese)

1 teaspoon minced fresh dill

1 teaspoon minced fresh chives, plus 1 bunch for decorating

1 teaspoon fresh lemon juice

½ large cucumber (about 5 ounces), very thinly sliced

4 ounces thinly sliced smoked salmon

Edible flowers, for decorating (see tip)

Using a paring knife, trim the pita as needed to ensure that the rounds are the same size. To do this, trim one and use it as a template for the others; don't worry if the breads are slightly cracked or uneven as this will be hidden by the cream cheese "frosting." Set the breads aside.

To make the filling, in a bowl, stir together 1 container cream cheese, ¼ cup of the fromage blanc, the dill, the 1 teaspoon minced chives, and the lemon juice until well combined.

Place one bread onto a flat round serving plate or platter. Using a small offset spatula or a mini rubber spatula, spread one-quarter of the cream cheese filling (about ¼ cup) in an even layer over the top of the bread. Top with half of the cucumber slices, placing them in an even layer and overlapping them in a decorative pattern. Top with a second bread, then spread ¼ cup of the cream cheese filling onto the bread. Top with half of the salmon, placing the slices in an even layer. Top with a third bread, ¼ cup cream cheese filling, and the remaining cucumber slices. Top with a fourth bread, the remaining cream cheese filling, and the remaining salmon slices. Top with the final bread and press the "cake" gently to make sure the top is even. ~ *Continued on page 82* ~

Be colorful

Use a variety of pesticide-free edible flowers, such as violets, pansies, culinary lavender, and/or rose petals.

~ Continued from page 80 ~

In a bowl, combine the remaining container cream cheese and ⅓ cup fromage blanc and stir vigorously until the mixture is smooth. Using a small offset spatula or a mini rubber spatula, spread the "frosting" all over the sides and top of the cake, making sure to fill in the gaps on the sides of the cake and covering the cake in an even layer.

To decorate, cut the 1 bunch chives into 3-to-4-inch-long pieces. Press the chives into the sides of the cake one by one so that they stick to the "frosting" and resemble grass. Decorate the cake with edible flowers. Cut into wedges and serve right away, or loosely cover with plastic wrap and refrigerate for up to 4 hours before serving.

Individual Chicken Pot Pies

This classic dish is always a hit, especially when it's served in individual portions at a cozy afternoon tea party. You can use homemade or store-bought pie dough, and using leftover rotisserie chicken makes quick work of assembling the filling.

Basic Pie Dough (page 117) or 2 sheets store-bought refrigerated piecrust

4 tablespoons (½ stick) unsalted butter

1 tablespoon olive oil

½ yellow onion, chopped

2 cups small broccoli florets

2 carrots, peeled and sliced

2 cloves garlic, minced

5 fresh sage leaves, chopped

Salt and ground black pepper

¼ cup all-purpose flour, plus more for dusting

2 cups chicken broth

½ cup half-and-half

2½ cups diced cooked chicken

1 large egg mixed with 1 tablespoon heavy cream

 Prepare the pie dough and chill as directed. If using store-bought dough, keep refrigerated until needed.

Preheat the oven to 375°F. In a large frying pan over medium-high heat, warm 1 tablespoon of the butter and the oil. Add the onion and cook, stirring often, until soft, about 8 minutes. Add the broccoli, carrots, garlic, and sage and season well with salt and pepper. Cook, stirring often, until the broccoli is bright green, about 2 minutes. Transfer to a large bowl. Return the pan to the stove, add the remaining 3 tablespoons butter and the flour, and cook, stirring, for 1 minute. Stir in the broth and the half-and-half. Bring to a simmer and cook, stirring often, until thickened, about 5 minutes. Remove from the heat, add the cooked chicken, then stir into the vegetable mixture. Season with salt and pepper.

Have ready six 4½-inch ramekins or similar baking dishes. Using a rolling pin, roll out 1 chilled dough disk on a lightly floured work surface into a 10-inch round about ⅛ inch thick. Cut out 3 rounds about ¼ inch larger than the ramekins. Repeat with the remaining dough disk to make a total of 6 rounds. Cut a few small slits in the center of each round to vent the steam. Divide the chicken mixture evenly among the ramekins. Place a dough round over each ramekin, pressing the dough against the rim to seal it.

Carefully transfer the ramekins to a rimmed cookie sheet. Using a pastry brush, brush the top of each pie with the egg wash. Bake until the crust is golden brown, 20 to 25 minutes. Remove from the oven and let cool for 5 minutes, then serve.

Fresh Tomato Tart

Heirloom tomatoes are grown in a rainbow of colors, from classic red and deep purple to bright yellow and orange. Make this super easy but very impressive tart in the summer, when heirloom tomatoes are in season, or use large ripe tomatoes if you can't find heirlooms.

All-purpose flour, for dusting

1 sheet store-bought frozen puff pastry, thawed overnight in the refrigerator

3 to 4 ripe red, orange, or yellow tomatoes, or a combination

FOR THE HERBED GOAT CHEESE

4 ounces goat cheese, at room temperature

2 tablespoons chopped fresh basil, plus whole basil leaves for garnish

2 tablespoons chopped fresh parsley

3 tablespoons heavy cream

Salt and ground black pepper

 Preheat the oven to 425°F. Line a rimmed cookie sheet with parchment paper.

Very lightly dust a work surface with flour. Lay the puff pastry on the surface and lightly dust the top with flour. Using a rolling pin, roll out the sheet to a 10-by-15-inch rectangle about ⅛ inch thick. Place the rectangle on the prepared cookie sheet and put it in the freezer to chill while you prepare the tomatoes and herbed goat cheese.

Slice the tomatoes into rounds. Set aside on a plate.

To make the herbed goat cheese, stir together the goat cheese, chopped basil, parsley, and cream in a small bowl. Season with salt and pepper.

Remove the pastry from the freezer. Using a sharp knife, cut a 1-inch border along the edges of the puff pastry, being careful not to cut more than halfway through the pastry. Prick the pastry inside of the border all over with a fork. Bake until the pastry is golden brown and flaky, 15 to 20 minutes. Remove from the oven and let cool on the cookie sheet on a wire rack.

Using an icing spatula or the back of a spoon, spread the herbed goat cheese carefully across the pastry. Arrange the tomato slices in overlapping rows on top. Sprinkle with salt and garnish with basil leaves. Cut into squares and serve.

Cheddar & Herb Scones

Although often served as a sweet treat, scones can be savory, too. Pairing Cheddar cheese and fresh green herbs is a colorful and delicious way to transform a basic recipe into a tea party–worthy dish. Using a dough cutter with scalloped edges makes for an extra-pretty presentation.

2 cups all-purpose flour, plus more for dusting

1 cup grated Cheddar cheese

3 tablespoons chopped fresh green herbs, such as chives, dill, or parsley

2 teaspoons baking powder

Salt and ground black pepper

½ cup (1 stick) cold unsalted butter, cut into chunks

1 large egg

¾ cup heavy cream or whole milk

Preheat the oven to 400°F. Line a cookie sheet with parchment paper.

In a large bowl, using a fork, stir together the flour, cheese, herbs, baking powder, 1 teaspoon salt, and ½ teaspoon pepper. Add the butter and toss it well to coat with the flour mixture. Using a pastry blender or 2 knives, cut the butter into the flour mixture until the mixture forms coarse crumbs the size of small peas. In a small bowl, whisk together the egg and cream until blended. Pour the egg mixture over the flour mixture and stir with the fork just until the dough comes together.

Sprinkle a work surface with flour. Dump the dough onto the floured surface. Form the dough into a ball. Using a floured rolling pin, roll out the dough into a circle about ½ inch thick. Using a 3-inch round cookie cutter, cut out circles of dough, pressing the cookie cutter straight down and lifting it straight up and spacing the circles as close together as possible. Place the dough rounds at least 2 inches apart on the cookie sheet. Gather up the dough scraps, knead them briefly together on the floured work surface, and roll out the dough again. Cut out more rounds using the cookie cutter and add them to the cookie sheet. You should have 12 scones.

Bake until the scones are golden brown, about 12 minutes. Transfer the scones from the cookie sheet to a wire rack to cool slightly. Serve warm.

Potato & Pea Samosas

While they're typically fried, samosas are baked in our version, using store-bought piecrust. A vegetarian filling of mashed potato and peas is traditional for this Indian snack, but once you get the hang of the process, try out other combinations of soft ingredients, such as cooked lentils or chickpeas.

1¼ pound russet potatoes (about 2 large), peeled and cut into 1-inch cubes

Salt and ground black pepper

2 tablespoons canola or vegetable oil

½ yellow onion, chopped

2 garlic cloves, minced or grated

2-inch piece fresh ginger, peeled and grated (about 1 teaspoon)

1 cup frozen peas

2 teaspoons ground coriander

1 teaspoon ground cumin

½ teaspoon garam masala

 Fill a large saucepan three-quarters full of water. Carefully add the potatoes and 1 tablespoon salt, stir, and bring to a boil over medium-high heat. Reduce heat to medium-low and simmer until the potatoes are tender and easily poked with a fork, 10 to 15 minutes. Drain the potatoes in a colander set in the sink, transfer to a large bowl, and set aside.

In a large frying pan over medium heat, warm the oil. Add the onion and cook, stirring occasionally, until lightly browned, about 5 minutes. Add the garlic and ginger and cook until fragrant, about 1 minute. Add the peas, coriander, cumin, garam masala, 1 teaspoon salt, and ⅛ teaspoon pepper and cook until softened, stirring occasionally, about 2 minutes. Add the reserved potatoes and cook until warmed through, about 2 minutes.

Return the mixture to the bowl, add the cilantro, and mix well, mashing the potatoes as you go.

Preheat the oven to 400°F. Line a cookie sheet with parchment paper.

¼ cup chopped fresh cilantro leaves

1 tablespoon all-purpose flour, plus more for dusting

1 large egg

3 sheets store-bought refrigerated piecrust

In a small bowl, stir together the flour and 2 tablespoons water. In another small bowl, whisk together the egg and 1 tablespoon water.

On a lightly floured work surface, roll out 1 sheet of piecrust until smooth and about ⅛ inch thick. Using a 4½-inch cutter (or a template made by tracing a large circle onto a piece of cardboard), cut out 4 circles from the dough as closely together as possible. Cut each circle in half to make 8 half-moons. Gently press the scraps together, reroll the dough, cut out 1 more circle, then cut it into 2 more half-moons, for a total of 10.

Place 1 tablespoon of the potato filling in the center of each half-moon. Dip your finger in the flour paste and run it along the edges of the dough. Fold the dough in half to make a cone shape. Press the edges gently to seal, tucking in the filling so it doesn't leak out. Use the tines of a fork to seal the edges. Transfer to the prepared cookie sheet and repeat to fill the remaining dough. Brush the top of each samosa with egg wash. Bake until golden brown and crisp, 12 to 15 minutes.

While the first batch bakes, repeat the process two more times for filling and baking the remaining sheets of dough. Serve warm.

Say cheese!
Not a fan of alpine cheeses? You can also use grated Cheddar, Monterey Jack, Parmesan, or another good melting cheese for these bites.

Cheese Gougères

One bite of these light and airy cheese puffs and you'll be hooked! The choux pastry batter can be made with any variety of the smooth and pungent alpine cheeses commonly found in France, where gougères first appeared on afternoon tea trays in the seventeenth century.

2 cups plus 2 tablespoons whole milk

½ cup (1 stick) unsalted butter

2 teaspoons salt

2 cups all-purpose flour

8 large eggs

½ pound Gruyère, Emmentaler, or other Swiss-type cheese, finely shredded

 Preheat the oven to 375°F. Line 2 cookie sheets with parchment paper.

In a heavy saucepan over high heat, combine 2 cups of the milk, the butter, and salt and bring to a boil. Add the flour all at once, reduce the heat to low, and stir with a wooden spoon or rubber spatula until the mixture forms a ball and pulls cleanly away from the sides of the pan, about 5 minutes. Remove from the heat, transfer to a large bowl, and let cool for 2 minutes.

Using an electric mixer on medium speed, add the eggs, one at a time, beating well after each addition until well mixed and the dough is very shiny; this step should take about 5 minutes. Stir in three-fourths of the cheese.

Using a spoon, scoop out rounds of dough 2 to 3 inches in diameter and place them on the prepared cookie sheets, spacing them about 2 inches apart. Brush the rounds with the remaining 2 tablespoons milk, then sprinkle evenly with the remaining cheese.

Bake the gougères until well puffed and golden brown, 30 to 35 minutes. Let them cool briefly on the cookie sheets on wire racks and serve warm, or let cool completely and serve at room temperature.

Pepperoni, Spinach & Tomato Deep-Dish Mini Pizzas

These super-cheesy bite-size pizzas are made in a muffin pan. You can prepare them ahead of time—just underbake them by 5 minutes, store them in a plastic bag in the refrigerator or freezer, then rewarm them in a 300°F oven until the crust is golden and the filling is warmed through, 5 to 10 minutes.

FOR THE PIZZA DOUGH

3¾ cups bread flour, plus more for dusting

⅔ cup cornmeal

1 package (2¼ teaspoons) quick-rise yeast

1½ tablespoons sugar

1 tablespoon salt

1½ cups warm (110°F) water, plus more as needed

5 tablespoons olive oil, plus more for greasing

To make the dough, in a food processor, combine the flour, cornmeal, yeast, sugar, and salt and pulse to mix. With the motor running, add the water and oil in a steady stream, then pulse until the dough comes together in a rough ball, about 12 seconds. If necessary, sprinkle with 1 to 2 teaspoons water and pulse again until a rough ball forms. Let rest for 5 to 10 minutes.

Process the dough again for 25 to 30 seconds, steadying the top of the processor with one hand. The dough should be tacky to the touch but not sticky. Transfer the dough to a lightly floured work surface and knead into a smooth ball. Place the dough in a large oiled bowl, turn the ball to coat it with oil, and cover the bowl with plastic wrap. Let rise in a warm place until doubled in size and spongy, about 2 hours.

Preheat the oven to 450°F. Brush the bottom of each cup in a standard 12-cup muffin pan with oil.

Rise to the occasion

Remember to leave enough time for the dough to rise (about 2 hours) before you assemble the pizzas.

1½ cups store-bought pizza sauce

Salt and ground black pepper

1 large tomato, chopped

2 cups fresh spinach leaves, chopped

3 ounces sliced pepperoni, chopped

1 cup shredded mozzarella cheese

Punch down the dough, then turn it out onto a lightly floured work surface and shape it into a smooth cylinder. Cut the dough in half. Let one half rest for 10 minutes; keep the other half for future use. (You can store the extra dough in a lock-top plastic bag. Refrigerate it for up to 1 day or freeze for up to 1 month, then bring it to room temperature before using.) Cut the dough into 12 equal pieces. Using a rolling pin, roll each piece into a 5-inch circle. Fit a dough circle into each prepared muffin cup. The dough should extend about ¼ inch over the top of each cup.

Spoon 1 tablespoon pizza sauce into each dough cup and season with salt and pepper. Fill each cup evenly with tomato, spinach, and pepperoni, then top with another tablespoon of pizza sauce and some shredded cheese. Bake until the pizzas are golden brown on the bottom and the cheese is melted, 12 to 14 minutes. Let cool for 5 minutes, then serve.

Sausage & Cheese Stuffed Mushrooms

When you are hosting a tea party, it's a good idea to serve a selection of flavorful finger foods that are easy to eat with your hands. These savory bites are the perfect addition to any menu. You can use classic white button or cremini mushrooms—just be sure to choose ones that are approximately the same size so they cook evenly.

1 tablespoon butter, at room temperature

24 large white or cremini mushrooms, caps left whole, stems removed and finely chopped

2 tablespoons olive oil

½ cup chopped yellow onion

Salt and ground black pepper

1 pound Italian sausage

8 ounces cream cheese, at room temperature

2 tablespoons chopped fresh flat-leaf parsley

½ teaspoon garlic salt

Preheat the oven to 350°F. Coat the bottom of an 8-by-10-inch baking dish with butter. Place the mushroom caps, gill sides up, in a single layer in the baking dish and set aside.

In a frying pan over medium-high heat, warm 1 tablespoon of the oil. Add the onion and chopped mushroom stems and season with salt and pepper. Sauté, stirring often, until soft, 6 to 8 minutes. Transfer to a large bowl. Return the frying pan to the stovetop over medium-high heat and warm the remaining 1 tablespoon oil. Add the sausage and cook, breaking up the meat with a wooden spoon, until browned, about 8 minutes. Transfer to the bowl with the onion mixture. Let cool for 5 minutes. Add the cream cheese, parsley, and garlic salt and mix until combined.

Generously stuff the mushroom caps with the filling. Bake until the mushrooms are soft and the filling is warmed through, 25 to 30 minutes. Let cool slightly, then serve.

Pigs in a Pretzel

Even tastier than the popular retro hors d'oeuvres called pigs in a blanket, these addictive snacks are super cute and fun to make. Prepare the pretzel dough as you would a bread dough, letting it rise in a warm place so the yeast can work its magic. Boiling and baking the dough makes it soft inside and crispy outside.

FOR THE DOUGH

1 cup warm (110°F) water

1 package (2¼ teaspoons) active dry yeast

1 tablespoon sugar

3 tablespoons olive oil

3¼ cups all-purpose flour, plus more for dusting

1 teaspoon kosher salt

Vegetable oil, for brushing

⅓ cup baking soda

14 hot dogs, each cut into 3 pieces, or 40 cocktail-size mini franks or sausages

Coarse salt, for sprinkling

Mustard of choice, for serving

To make the dough, in the bowl of a stand mixer, stir together the warm water, yeast, and sugar. Let stand until foamy, about 10 minutes. Add the olive oil, flour, and kosher salt. Attach the dough hook and knead the dough on medium-low speed until smooth, about 10 minutes. Form the dough into a ball, cover the bowl with plastic wrap, and let rise in a warm spot until doubled in bulk, about 1 hour.

Preheat the oven to 450°F. Line 2 cookie sheets with parchment paper and brush the parchment with vegetable oil. Fill a large, wide saucepan with 7 cups water, stir in the baking soda, and bring to a boil over high heat.

Cut the dough in half. On a lightly floured work surface, using a rolling pin, roll one half of the dough into a 6-by-10-inch rectangle. Cut the dough crosswise into ten 1-inch-wide strips, then cut the strips in half so that they are 3 inches long.

Lay a piece of hot dog onto each piece of dough and wrap the dough around the hot dog, leaving the ends of the hot dog exposed. Pinch the ends of the dough firmly to seal them together. Repeat the process with the other half of the dough. Working in batches, if necessary, gently lower the pigs into the boiling water and cook for 1 minute. Use a large slotted spoon to carefully transfer them to the prepared cookie sheets. Sprinkle the pigs with coarse salt.

Bake until deep brown, 10 to 12 minutes. Serve right away, with mustard.

Rainbow Sushi

These cone-shaped hand rolls are a fun and easy way to get started making sushi. Fill a sheet of nori (made of dried seaweed) with sushi rice and a colorful combination of matchstick veggies, then roll it into a cone for easy eating with your hands.

FOR THE SUSHI RICE

2 tablespoons rice vinegar

1½ tablespoons sugar

½ tablespoon salt

1 cup short-grain white rice

FOR ASSEMBLING THE ROLLS

1 teaspoon rice vinegar

3 sheets nori, cut in half

1 tablespoon toasted sesame seeds

½ English cucumber, peeled and cut into matchsticks

1 carrot, peeled and cut into matchsticks

1 ripe avocado, pitted, peeled, and thinly sliced

Low-sodium soy sauce and pickled ginger, for serving (optional)

To make the sushi rice, combine the vinegar, sugar, and salt in a small saucepan. Set the pan over low heat and cook, stirring, until the sugar and salt dissolve, about 2 minutes. Let cool completely.

Place the white rice in a large fine-mesh sieve and rinse under running cold water until the water runs clear. Drain well. Transfer the rice to a medium heavy-bottomed saucepan and pour in 1½ cups water. Set the pan over medium heat and bring to a boil, stir once, and reduce the heat to low. Cover the pan with a tight-fitting lid and cook, without opening the lid, until the rice is tender and has absorbed all the water, about 15 minutes. Turn off the heat and let sit for 5 minutes. Using a fork, fluff the rice.

Put the hot cooked rice in a large baking dish and use a spatula to spread it out evenly. Slowly pour in the vinegar mixture while slicing the spatula through the rice; flip the rice with the spatula to mix in the vinegar mixture, but do not stir it. Cover the dish with a clean, damp kitchen towel until ready to use.

To assemble the hand rolls, combine the vinegar with 2 tablespoons water in a small bowl. Place 1 piece of nori, shiny side down, on a clean, dry work surface with a long side closest to you. Scoop about ¼ cup of the seasoned rice onto the left third of the nori. Lightly moisten your fingers with the vinegar-water mixture and gently flatten the rice; don't let the rice spread too much or cover the corners. Lightly sprinkle the rice with ½ teaspoon sesame seeds and place a few pieces of cucumber, carrot, and avocado diagonally on the rice, angled up to the far-left corner of the nori. Lift the bottom left corner of the nori, bring it up over the fillings, and begin rolling, forming a point at the bottom right edge of the rice; keep rolling until the nori forms a cone around the fillings. Very lightly moisten the seam with the vinegar-water mixture to seal it. Set the hand roll on a platter. Repeat with the remaining ingredients. Serve the hand rolls with soy sauce and pickled ginger, if you like.

Drinks

Frozen Chai

What could be better than a spicy cup of tea full of rich flavors? A flavor-packed milkshake topped with whipped cream and a sprinkle of cinnamon! Prepare a warming pot of hot chai, then transform it into a frozen treat by blending it with ice cream.

4 cups whole milk

4 bags chai tea

10 peppercorns

3 slices fresh ginger

2 tablespoons sugar

1 pint vanilla ice cream, softened

Whipped Cream (page 115)

Ground cinnamon, for sprinkling

In a medium saucepan over medium-high heat, warm the milk just until steam begins to rise. Remove from the heat and add the tea bags, peppercorns, ginger, and sugar. Stir briefly to dissolve the sugar. Let cool to room temperature, remove the tea bags, then transfer to an airtight container and chill for at least 2 hours or up to overnight.

Pour the chai through a fine-mesh sieve into a blender. Add the ice cream and process until smooth. Pour into 4 glasses, top each with a dollop of whipped cream, sprinkle with cinnamon and serve.

Keep it whole
Make sure you use
only whole black
peppercorns for this
spicy concoction. Using
ground pepper will
make your drink
taste bitter.

Masala Chai

This tea will warm you from the inside out. Steep the milk, spices, and tea bags in a saucepan with a lip for easy pouring into mugs. You can find cardamom pods in the spice aisle of the grocery store or online, but if you can't locate any, replace them with 1 teaspoon of ground cardamom.

4 cups whole milk

6 cardamom pods

1 cinnamon stick

8 black peppercorns

4 whole cloves

3 black tea bags

½ cup sugar

In a medium saucepan over medium-high heat, combine the milk, cardamom, cinnamon, peppercorns, and cloves and bring to a boil. Reduce heat to low and simmer, uncovered, for 10 minutes. Add the tea bags, cover, and steep over low heat for 5 minutes. Remove the tea bags. Stir in the sugar until it is dissolved, and remove from the heat.

Pour the milk through a fine-mesh sieve directly into 4 mugs and serve hot.

Matcha Latte

Matcha is a bright green Japanese green-tea powder made from dried tea leaves. You'll need to whisk the powder into the water and milk quickly and vigorously to create the right amount of foam (you can use a special matcha whisk, called a chasen, for this step), so it's easiest to make this colorful latte one cup at a time.

¼ teaspoon matcha powder

¼ cup boiling water

¾ cup steamed milk, such as whole milk, almond milk, coconut milk, or oat milk

Honey, for sweetening (optional)

 Sift the matcha powder into a mug. (This will break up any lumps in the powder.)

Pour the boiling water into the mug and whisk vigorously from side to side until all of the powder is dissolved and a layer of foam appears on top. Add the steamed milk and whisk again until foamy.

Taste and add a few drops of honey to sweeten it, if you like.

Keep it real

For a traditional cup of matcha, replace the ¾ cup steamed milk with boiling water.

Mint Tisane

By adding fresh mint leaves to a pot of hot water, you create a refreshing, aromatic herbal tea that's perfect for any tea party, or for an energizing way to start the day. Add a few bunches of lemon verbena to the pot along with the mint for an even more flavorful cup.

2 bunches fresh mint, washed and dried

Sugar, for serving (optional)

Put the mint in a teapot. In a teakettle or small saucepan, bring 6 cups water to a boil over high heat. Pour the water into the teapot and let steep for 3 minutes for a mild-flavored tisane or up to 5 minutes for a stronger mint flavor.

Pour the tisane through a tea strainer or fine-mesh sieve into cups or mugs. Serve right away, passing sugar at the table, if you like.

Strawberry-Coconut Boba Tea

Using rainbow tapioca pearls makes this fruity, tropical iced drink even more colorful. Add white or green tea for a lighter drink or leave it out for a smoothie-like texture. Then top each glass with a tiny strawberry and a straw in a pretty pattern.

1 cup tapioca pearls

2 tablespoons maple syrup or honey

2 cups frozen strawberries

1 cup unsweetened coconut milk

½ cup water or coconut water

3 tablespoons sweetened condensed milk

Ice, for serving

2 cups chilled white or green tea, home brewed (see tip) or store-bought (optional)

Small fresh strawberries, for serving (optional)

In a large saucepan over medium-high heat, bring 10 cups water to a boil. Slowly add the tapioca pearls and stir gently. Cook until tapioca floats to the top of the water, about 45 seconds, then cover and cook over medium heat for 2 to 3 minutes. Turn off the heat and let stand for 2 to 3 minutes.

Make an ice bath by filling a large bowl with ice and water. Drain the tapioca in a colander set in the sink (or scoop the balls out of the saucepan using a mesh sieve) and transfer to the ice bath. Let the tapioca balls cool for 30 seconds in the ice bath, then drain them again and transfer them to a clean, dry bowl. While they are still warm, toss them with the maple syrup.

In a blender, combine the frozen strawberries, coconut milk, water, and condensed milk and blend until creamy and smooth.

In each of 4 tall glasses, place ¼ cup cooked tapioca pearls. Add a handful of ice to each glass. Top each with ½ cup tea, if you like. Divide the strawberry mixture evenly among the glasses, and serve with a colorful straw. Top with a small strawberry, if you like.

Brew master

To brew your own white or green tea, place 2 tea bags in a large measuring jug or pitcher. Add 2 cups boiling water and let steep for 3 to 5 minutes. Remove tea bags, let cool, and refrigerate until ready to use.

Apple-Orange Tea with Blueberry Ice Cubes

Here's a frosty, fruity tea perfect for summer days. This recipe calls for blueberry ice cubes, but you can use your favorite berries instead. Make sure not to let the tea steep for too long, or it will turn bitter.

2 red apples, quartered and cored

1 orange, quartered

1 cinnamon stick

2 whole cloves

4 tablespoons black tea leaves

Blueberry ice cubes (page 119)

Sugar or honey, for sweetening

In a saucepan over medium-high heat, combine the fruit quarters, cinnamon, cloves, tea leaves, and 4 cups water and bring to a boil. Remove from the heat and let stand for 30 minutes. Strain the mixture through a sieve into a pitcher or jug, pressing on the fruit to extract all the flavor. Let cool to room temperature. Fill 4 glasses with blueberry ice cubes and pour in the tea. Sweeten with sugar or honey as desired.

Basics

White Chocolate Frosting

MAKES ABOUT 1 CUP

2 ounces white
chocolate,
finely chopped

¼ cup (½ stick)
unsalted butter,
at room temperature

1¼ cups powdered sugar

1½ tablespoons
whole milk

¼ teaspoon
vanilla extract

Pinch of salt

About ½ teaspoon
pink or orange gel food
coloring (optional)

 Put the chocolate in a small microwave-safe bowl and microwave for 25 seconds. Stir and continue to microwave, stopping to stir every 15 seconds, just until melted and smooth. Let cool for about 10 minutes.

In a large bowl, using an electric mixer, beat the butter on medium speed until light and fluffy, about 2 minutes. Turn off the mixer and scrape down the bowl with a rubber spatula. Add the powdered sugar, milk, vanilla, salt, and food coloring, if using, and beat on medium speed until combined. Add the white chocolate and beat until fully combined. Turn off the mixer and scrape down the bowl with the spatula. On medium-high speed, beat until fluffy and smooth, about 5 minutes.

If not using immediately, store the frosting in an airtight container in the refrigerator for up to 2 days. Stir vigorously just before using.

Even melting
When melting chocolate in the microwave, be sure to stir it every 15 seconds so it melts evenly.

Cream Cheese Frosting

MAKES ABOUT 1½ CUPS

1 (8-ounce) package cream cheese, at room temperature

6 tablespoons (¾ stick) unsalted butter, at room temperature

1 teaspoon vanilla extract

1 cup powdered sugar (plus 1 cup if you will be using a piping bag; see tip)

 In a large bowl, using an electric mixer, beat the cream cheese, butter, and vanilla on medium-high speed until light and fluffy, about 2 minutes. Turn off the mixer and scrape down the bowl with a rubber spatula. Add about half of the powdered sugar and mix on low speed until well blended. Turn off the mixer, add the remaining sugar, then beat on medium speed until smooth. The frosting should be spreadable; if it is too soft, cover the bowl and refrigerate it for about 15 minutes.

Easy piping
If you will be piping this frosting instead of spreading it, double the amount of powdered sugar to make it easier to work with in the piping bag.

Fluffy Frosting

MAKES ABOUT 2 CUPS

½ cup (1 stick)
unsalted butter,
at room temperature

2½ cups powdered sugar

3 tablespoons whole milk

1 teaspoon vanilla extract

Pinch of salt

In a large bowl, using an electric mixer, beat the butter on medium speed until light and fluffy, about 2 minutes. Turn off the mixer. Add the powdered sugar, milk, vanilla, and salt. Mix on low speed just until combined. Stop the mixer and scrape down the bowl with a rubber spatula. Beat on medium-high speed until the frosting is airy and smooth, about 5 minutes.

Variation

Fluffy Mint Frosting: Add ½ teaspoon peppermint extract with the vanilla extract.

Whipped Cream

MAKES ABOUT 1 CUP

1 cup heavy cream

2 tablespoons sugar

½ teaspoon
vanilla extract

In a bowl, using an electric mixer fitted with the whisk attachment, whip the cream, sugar, and vanilla on medium speed until medium peaks form, about 3 minutes. Do not overbeat, or you will end up with butter! Use right away or cover with plastic wrap and refrigerate until ready to use, up to 4 hours. Whisk the whipped cream briefly before using.

Basic Tart Dough

MAKES ENOUGH DOUGH FOR 1 TART

1 large egg yolk

1 teaspoon vanilla extract

2 tablespoons ice water

1¼ cups all-purpose flour

¼ cup sugar

½ teaspoon salt

½ cup (1 stick) cold unsalted butter, cut into small cubes

 In a small bowl or measuring jug, whisk together the egg yolk, vanilla, and water.

In the bowl of a food processor, combine the flour, sugar, and salt. Sprinkle the butter over the top and pulse for a few seconds, or just until the butter is broken up into the flour. Pour the egg mixture over the flour mixture, then pulse just until the mixture starts to come together.

Dump the dough into a large lock-top plastic bag and press into a flat disk. Refrigerate for at least 30 minutes and up to 1 day before using, or freeze for up to 1 month.

Cream Cheese Tart Dough

MAKES ENOUGH DOUGH FOR 1 TART

½ cup (1 stick) unsalted butter, at room temperature

3 ounces cream cheese, at room temperature

1 cup all-purpose flour, plus more for dusting

 In the bowl of a stand mixer fitted with the paddle attachment, or using a large bowl and an electric mixer, beat the butter and cream cheese on low speed until smooth and blended, about 45 seconds. Add the flour and mix until a smooth dough forms. Transfer the dough to a lightly dusted work surface and shape into a thick log. Wrap with plastic wrap and store in the refrigerator until ready to use, or for up to 3 days.

Basic Pie Dough

MAKES ENOUGH DOUGH FOR ONE 9-INCH PIE

2 cups all-purpose flour

1 tablespoon sugar

½ teaspoon salt

¾ cup (1½ sticks) cold unsalted butter, cut into small cubes

½ cup ice water, plus more if needed

In the bowl of a food processor, combine the flour, sugar, and salt. Sprinkle the butter over the top and pulse for a few seconds, or just until the butter is slightly broken up into the flour but still in visible pieces. Evenly sprinkle the water over the flour mixture, then pulse just until the mixture starts to come together. If needed, add a few more drops of water and pulse until the mixture comes together.

Dump the dough into a large lock-top plastic bag and press into a flat disk. Refrigerate for at least 30 minutes and up to 1 day before using, or freeze for up to 1 month.

Be creative
Try sprigs of herbs, colorful edible flowers, and a mixture of berries to create these little works of art. You can also use star-shaped ice cube molds and fill them with multicolored fruit juices.

Fruity Ice Cubes

MAKES 25 ICE CUBES

1½ quarts distilled water

Berries, such as blueberries

Fill a saucepan with the distilled water. Set the pan over high heat and bring to a boil. Remove from the heat and set aside to cool completely. (Distilled water has fewer impurities than tap water, and boiling it creates clear, rather than cloudy, ice cubes.)

Using 2 or more berries per cube depending on how big they are, place the berries in an even layer on a small tray and freeze until solid before using.

Fill each ice cube mold with some of the cooled distilled water so it comes about a third of the way up the mold. Place a few berries into each cube. Place the ice cube tray in the freezer and freeze until firm (but not solid). Put the rest of the distilled water in the refrigerator while the cubes set.

Remove the tray from the freezer and add a little more water, filling each mold again about a third of the way (don't be tempted to overfill it or it will melt and the berry will float). Gently push the berry down if it floats. Put the ice cube tray back in the freezer and freeze the next layer until firm. Top off each ice cube mold with water to fill it to the top. Return to the freezer and freeze until firm. You can keep the ice cubes in the mold or remove them and put them in a bowl and then use the molds to make more.

Index

weldonowen

PO Box 3088 San Rafael, CA 94912
www.weldonowen.com

WELDON OWEN
Publisher Roger Shaw
VP of Sales Julie Hamilton

Associate Publisher Amy Marr
Editorial Director Katie Killebrew
Editorial Assistant Jourdan Plautz

VP of Creative Chrissy Kwasnik
Designer Megan Sinead Harris
Production Managers Greg Steffen and Sam Taylot
VP of Manufacturing Alix Nicholaeff
Imaging Manager Don Hill

Photographer Nicole Hill Gerulat
Food Stylist Karen Evans
Prop Stylists Taylor Olson and Veronica Olson

AMERICAN GIRL *TEA PARTIES*
Conceived and produced by Weldon Owen International

A WELDON OWEN PRODUCTION

Printed and bound in China

First printed in 2021
10 9 8 7 6 5 4 3 2

Library of Congress Cataloging in Publication
data is available

ISBN 13: 978-1-68188-759-3

ACKNOWLEDGMENTS
Weldon Owen wishes to thank the following people for their generous support to help produce this book:
Taylor Bateman, Lesley Bruynesteyn, Milan Cook, Rachel Markowitz,
Emily Munk, A'Lissa Olson, Elizabeth Parson, and Brennan Stratton

A VERY SPECIAL THANK YOU TO:
Our models: Indiana DeVere, Evie Gerulat, Savannah Lawrence, Naomi Maughan,
Aida Nielsen, Penelope Reynolds, Tatum Smith, and Leilani Sun

Our locations: Highland Gardens and The Gerulats

Collect Them All

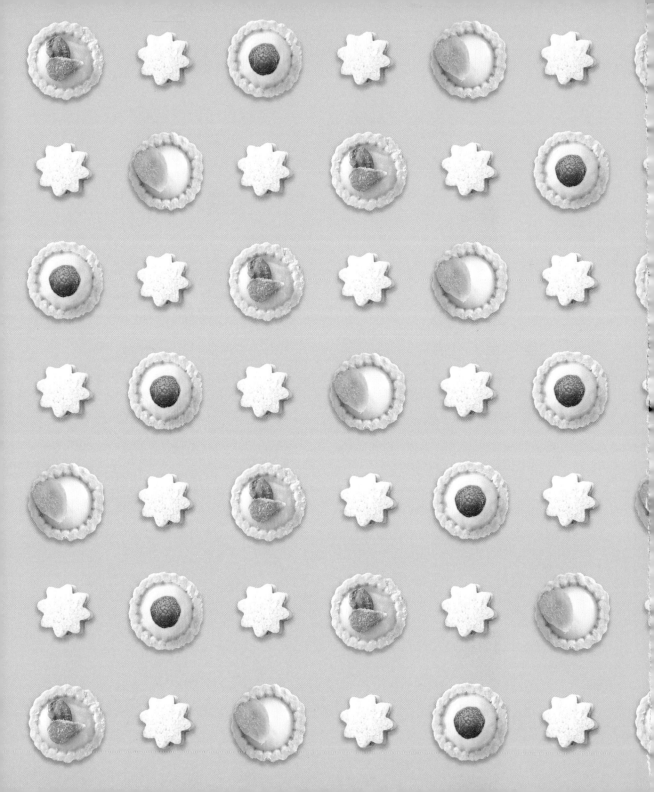